Getting To Know Dakota

An Insiders Guide to North Dakota

Volume Five
North Dakota Centennial Series

Published by
The Dakota Graphic Society
Fargo, North Dakota

Text: Nancy Edmonds Hanson
Photographs: Sheldon Green
Russ Hanson
Production: Leonard Roehrich
Historical photographs: State Historical Society
of North Dakota.
Printer: Knight Printing Company, Fargo.

Dakota Graphic Society
Box 9199
Fargo, North Dakota 58109

In the Pembina Hills on a fall afternoon, one of the joys of traveling the highways of North Dakota.

CONTENTS

1

Getting To Know Dakota

Those who know North Dakota best know her through her byways.

Like the lines on the palm of a hand, that network of roads — from river to railway to cow path to four-lane — reflects the fortunes of the 39th state and has often dictated its destiny.

Once buffalo cut trails across the high plains, followed by Indians and traders and hunters. Canoes and barges and steamboats paddled powerful prairie rivers. Advancing railroads marked the progress of industrial America across an uncharted land.

But for most of the single century since statehood, highways have tethered North Dakota to its neighbors, and tethered villages, farms and cities to the state as a whole. That's how Dakotans relate to the land. And that's how visitors come to know Dakota — be they native-born sons and daughters coming home from far away, or modern-day immigrants, or lifelong Dakota residents inspired by the centennial to explore beyond the limits of their daily routine.

In **Getting To Know Dakota** we've set out to weave together history (both documented and fanciful), the natural state, and bits of contemporary living...the whole rough and appealing fabric that reflects North Dakota values, pleasures and habits.

We've spun these yarns from an accumulation of sources, both personal observations and borrowed from a liberal assortment of literature ranging from chamber of commerce publications to newspaper stories, from roadside monuments to well-told anecdotes, from *Horizons Magazine* to the priceless collections of the Institute for Regional Studies.

Much information comes from earlier published sources detailed in the bibliography. Several books must be singled out for major contributions, not only to this project but to countless other books and accounts of North Dakota: *North Dakota, A Guide to the Northern Prairie State*, a publication of the Federal Writers Project of the Works Progress Administration first published in 1938; *Origins of North Dakota Place Names* by Mary Ann Barnes Williams, published by the author in 1966; and Elwyn B. Robinson's *History of North Dakota*, the most valuable of all accounts of the state from conception and birth through middle age.

We have attempted to verify the material in this book by confirming it through more than one source. That's not always possible, given the frequent contradictions among published accounts and the rather apocryphal nature of many matters which conventional wisdom today accepts as fact. Never have we let doubt interfere with a good story!

Getting To Know Dakota, finally, is an unfinished work. We invite you to share information on your favorite points of interest, beauty spots and bits of history. They'll be included in future editions of this book.

In the meantime, get out your road map, gas up the car and prepare to hit the road in search of the real North Dakota. It's a subtle and surprising pursuit that can occupy a lifetime.

About Using This Book: Getting To Know Dakota is organized into six driving tours, each beginning from and ending in one of the state's larger cities. We've attempted to give priority to the most heavily traveled routes, with side trips and alternate highways connecting these major roads.

If your path varies considerably from these, we hope the index on the last pages of this book assist you in charting your own course.

Numbers in parentheses following the initial mention of each city's name refer to its population according to 1980 U.S. Census data.

Agricultural Capital of the World

The Highlights: Explore the agricultural bounty of the southern Red River Valley, once the site of the gigantic early Industrial Age wheat factories called "bonanza farms" and now (along with the northern portion of the valley) a region that lays strong and literal claim to the title of Agricultural Capital of the World.

The Route: Beginning at Fargo, head west along Interstate 94 to Valley City. Then turn south on N.D. 32, with a side trip down the picturesque Sheyenne River Valley. Head east via N.D. 46 or — closer to the South Dakota line — either N.D. 13 or N.D. 11, incorporating a visit to Wahpeton. All three west-to-east routes bring you to Interstate 29, completing the tour with the drive back to Fargo. (The northern two-thirds of the Red River Valley, along with the Devils Lake area, is explored in Tour 6: Roots and the River/Grand Forks.)

Welcome to **Fargo**, North Dakota's largest city (with a 1980 population of 61,383) and the dominant center of the state's trade, finance and distribution, along with major medical and educational services.

The August 1988 issue of *Money Magazine* rated Fargo (with its sister city of Moorhead, Minn.) as the 38th best spot to live in America. Not only that: It's a nice place to visit, too.

With a metropolitan population of more than 100,000, Fargo-Moorhead offers North Dakota's broadest range of choices — in entertainment, the arts, shopping, special events, dining and accommodations.

Conceived by the Northern Pacific Railroad and delivered by an ambitious gaggle of land speculators and mercantile wizards, the wide-open circumstances of its youth contrast with the peaceful perspective of manicured lawns and prosperous commerce it offers today.

During its earliest years Fargo was schizophrenic. Its identity was shared by Fargo on the Prairie, a well-regimented encampment of soldiers protecting the Northern Pacific Railroad's construction crews, and Fargo in the Timber, a band of ragtag squatters so hell-bent on stretching the rules that a U.S. marshal led a contingent of soldiers up from Fort Abercrombie to rout them...not once, but twice.

That split personality persisted until the turn of the century. On the one hand, Fargo became known as the Divorce Capital of North America due to North Dakota's lax residency requirements. The rich and famous arrived in specially appointed Pullman cars, spending their time while divesting themselves of spouses in lavish entertainment at local opera houses and the several plush hotels furnished for such aristocratic guests.

Less rich, less famous but even more notorious were the denizens of riverfront establishments on both sides of the Red River. North Dakota entered the Union as a dry state, so Moorhead had the bootleggers, while Fargo hosted the red light district — not far from the site of today's police headquarters.

On the other hand, canny businessmen and clear-eyed reformers were building the prototype of a decent mid-American city, with its bustling Broadway and Front Street, its tree-lined streets, its churches and schools and parks. Testimony to their vision of civic pride survives in a spectacular park system, neighborhoods of handsome homes, and a variety of attractive sites and events.

It's hard to overplay the importance of railroads to Fargo's and North Dakota's history. Two reminders anchor the city's downtown district — the decaying Great Northern Depot on North Broadway (soon due for renovation) and the Northern Pacific Depot on Main Avenue. The latter, which houses the city's visitor information center, has been restored to its original romanesque glory. Its flower-bedecked plaza and fountain have regained their turn-of-the-century status as a local landmark.

Two much-debated statues are only a stone's throw away. At the foot of Broadway, Luis Jimenez's fiberglass ox and plowman strain to break the tough, hard sod. More abstract is *Dedication to a Birthplace*, a

5

Trollwood Park on Fargo's north side is an outdoor playground combining weekend arts festivals with the flavor of an old-time county fair. The area's musicians, dancers, jugglers and other performers take their turn on the outdoor stage during summer weekends. Crafts and art fairs are popular, as are rides on a stagecoach drawn by a team of Clydesdale horses. (Left) The street leading into Lindenwood Park has been renamed Roger Maris Drive, in honor of the native son who broke baseball's most cherished record, Babe Ruth's single-season home run record. Maris brought several of his Yankee teammates to Fargo for a charity golf tournament, like Hall of Famer Mickey Mantle, before his death from cancer in 1986. The tournament still attracts celebrities from the sports-world to Fargo each summer.

three-dimensional exploration of how the Red River joins and divides Fargo-Moorhead created by Lowell Reiland, a Wahpeton-born artist earning accolades on the national scene.

Fargo's park system offers a variety of experiences, from picnics and camping to sports and — perhaps uniquely — the arts. Two riverside areas are especially noteworthy: Trollwood and Lindenwood Parks.

Trollwood (on the north side) comes to life each weekend in summer with crafters showing their wares, vendors hawking Coke and cotton candy, and continuous music, drama and dance. Themes for the festivities range from a salute to Scandinavia to country music, hot-air ballooning and magic, as well as a mammoth outdoor Christmas bazaar during the last weekend of August.

The resident Trollwood Performing Arts School annually attracts hundreds of teenagers with a summer curriculum taught by seasoned professionals. It climaxes in July with an outdoor musical production — anything from "The King and I" to "The Wiz."

The second notable park is the more traditional Lindenwood, with its playgrounds, shady picnic areas and RV campground along Roger Maris Drive, so named in honor of the famous Fargo native who made baseball history by breaking Babe Ruth's record with 61 homes runs. Other tributes to him are scattered throughout the community, from the annual Roger Maris Charity Golf Tournament to the Roger Maris Museum at West Acres Shopping Center, which displays his New York Yankee uniform and other memorabilia from his career.

Two more park district projects rate mention: The Children's Museum at Yunker Farm, a new "please touch" experience for youngsters housed on a century-old farmstead, and Santa's Village. The latter is part of the annual Merry Prairie Christmas celebration in December, with sleigh rides, a pen of reindeer and a real Santa ho-ho-hoing for the young.

Fargo boasts a variety of arts groups, from the Red River Dance and Performing Company and F-M Symphony to the North Dakota Repertory Theatre each summer. The Plains Art Museum and the Rourke Gallery are located just across the river.

North Dakota State University has played a pivotal role in North Dakota's farm economy since it opened its doors in 1890. Its Experiment Station has pioneered new varieties of wheat, potatoes, sunflowers, barley and other crops; today the Northern Crops Institute, also headquartered on campus, hosts international delegations interested in making the best use of premium wheat from the prairie. The school has earned high marks in other areas as well, beginning with the work of Dr. Edwin Ladd, one of the nation's leading crusaders for pure foods (later NDSU president and U.S. senator). Modern examples include research in polymers and coatings, the Perkins Center for Technology Transfer...and football.

Though other firms now dominate its economy, **West Fargo** (10,099) owes it beginnings to Armour and Company. The national meat packer operated a large plant there from the 1920s through 1959, laying the groundwork for the city with company-owned worker housing.

Other companies have long since taken over the city's industrial future and that of Riverside just to the north. Among them are Red

The revitalized Northern Pacific Depot in downtown Fargo once again vibrates with activity. Now part office building, part gathering place, the grounds offer a shaded rest with an occasional concert on a warm summer's evening.

7

River Manufacturing, which sells live-bottom trailers to clients in construction, mining and agriculture; Prairie Products, which produces a line of snack foods including Dakota Kid sunflower seeds, and Northwest Professional Color, a professional photographic laboratory.

West Fargo's major attractions are Bonanzaville USA and the Red River Valley Fairgrounds. The Cass County Historical Society sponsors Bonanzaville, a prairie village circa 1900 built with more than 40 fully furnished homes and establishments gathered from sites throughout Cass County. Along with major collections of farm equipment, antique cars and airplanes, it houses outstanding exhibits of dolls and toys, Indian artifacts and household furnishings and equipment from throughout the settlement period.

During Pioneer Days (the third full weekend in August), that history is brought to life with hundreds of demonstrations of homestead-era skills, parades of antique automobiles and horse-drawn buggies, a threshing bee, Ladies Aid cuisine and old-time church services in Norwegian, German and Latin.

The fairgrounds' biggest event may be the Red River Valley Fair in mid-July, but that's not all. Big Iron, held in September, boasts one of the nation's leading farm equipment shows, built around what's biggest, most powerful and newest in the world of farm implements.

West of West Fargo on Interstate 94 is **Mapleton** (306), a site on the most popular ox cart route between Fort Garry and St. Paul and one of the first towns to be organized in North Dakota. In 1960 John Steinbeck paused here in his **Travels with Charley.** Nearby is the farm of former U.S. Senator and Congressman Mark Andrews.

Casselton (1,661) may have wielded more political clout on a per capita basis than any other North Dakota city. Three North Dakota governors — William Langer (later a U.S. senator), William Guy and George Sinner, all

Sprawling on several acres in West Fargo, Bonanzaville USA (opposite page & above) recalls a prairie village circa 1900, with major collections of farm equipment, antique cars and airplanes, and household furnishings from North Dakota's settlement period. In December, families greet the holiday season singing Christmas carols beneath bright strings of lights on the reconstructed Main Steet.

10   *The agricultural wealth produced in the fertile Red River Valley is characterized by this large Richland County farm.*

honored at Governors Park. The 19th century buildings of the downtown area are on the National Register of Historic Places.

Here was the unofficial capital of North Dakota's bonanza farm belt. These mammoth farms were the state of the agricultural art in the 1870s and early 1880s, when eastern investors (who acquired their acreage at fire-sale prices from the bankrupt Northern Pacific Railway Company) applied the principles of the Industrial Revolution to the labor-intensive craft of farming.

Casselton was headquarters for the mammoth Oliver Dalrymple farm, which by 1895 encompassed 65,000 acres (or more than 100 square miles) in Cass and Traill Counties. Dalrymple is thought to have introduced North Dakota to that newfangled contraption, the telephone; by 1876 he was using it to keep in touch with his distant foremen.

Among other local points of interest are a striking fieldstone church constructed by early Episcopalians but later occupied by other faiths, and what was once the most peculiar landmark along old Highway 10: a slightly skewed 100-foot tower constructed entirely of oil cans.

Traveling north of Casselton on ND #18 brings you first to **Amenia** (93), once the site of the most famous of the bonanza farms, the Amenia Sharon Land Company, named for towns in New York and Connecticut. Owned by a group of 36 investors, both the company and the settlement of Amenia were run by manager Eben Chaffee and his colleagues, who laid out the townsite around a central square reminiscent of villages back east. The Chaffee family's gift of an elegant town hall on the square went awry when the clan's matriarch discovered townspeople intended to use it for dancing. She disapproved. It was boarded up and remains so to this day. While the land company was disbanded in 1920, its vast horse stables and barracks for laborers survived into the late 1960s.

Arthur (446), originally called Rosedale, was named for Vice President Chester Arthur one year after he succeeded slain U.S. President James Garfield in 1881. Today Arthur is the home of Starr Fireworks, a manufacturer of exhibition fireworks whose credits include Expo '86, the Statue of Liberty celebration, the Texas Sesquicentennial and displays at Disneyworld. Its plant is one of largest, safest and most modern plants in the United States. Residents have grown accustomed to the rockets' red glare, since test firings are scheduled each Wednesday night.

The best-known resident of early **Hunter** (369) was pioneer homesteader and early bonanza farmer D.H. Houston, credited by many with the invention of the roll-film camera in 1881. He soldhis patent to George Eastman. Some believe that the name Kodak was built from the then-popular abbreviation "No. Dak." Houston also developed an improved wheat variety and patented improvements on the disc plow. One wing of his farm home, which boasted all the latest improvements of its day, is now incorporated into Bonanzaville USA in West Fargo.

The tallest structure in North America connects the prairie with the clouds north of Hunter. It's the broadcast tower of KTHI Television, with an official height of 2,063 feet.

Turn east at **Blanchard** to connect with Interstate 29 and other bonanza era communities including **Kelso**, **Grandin** (210) and **Gardner** (94). Prominent from territorial times as a grain shipping point, Grandin credits its identity to the Grandin brothers of Pennsylvania, who eventually acquired nearly 100,000 acres of railroad land for one of the most famous bonanza farms. Wheat was barged from here to Fargo on the Red River, 35 miles away by land but 90 miles by water.

Unlike the countless towns named for family roots, native lands, girlfriends and wives, or railroad officials, **Argusville** (147) owes its name to a newspaper — the Fargo **Daily**

The dreams by railroad promoters for eastern North Dakota have today come true...the land has produced a "Garden of Eden" of agricultural wealth and crop diversity. Flying over the flat checkerboard of ripening crops and neat farms is both educational and breathtaking.

Argus. The newspaper in turns owes its inspiration to the Greek mythological figure of Argus, the watchman with 100 eyes. Its modern heir, The Forum of Fargo-Moorhead, still bears a sign of that lineage: Its mail address is Box 20-20.

Fargo real estate dealer A.J. Harwood owned the townsite christened **Harwood** along with Almond White and Solomon Comstock, associates of the Great Northern Railway's James J. Hill and prominent as developers of towns throughout his empire. Today Hill, who dreamed of a Garden of Eden in the Great Northwest, might be pleased with the practical work done by horticulturist Neal Holland. Long associated with plant research at North Dakota State University, Holland now operates the picturesque Sheyenne Gardens nursery on his richly landscaped homestead northwest of town.

Continuing west from Casselton on I-94 are two names of much history but little imagination — **Wheatland** and **Buffalo** (226). Long-distance drivers owe Buffalo and one of its neighbors for providing the most-noticed exit on the interstate, "Buffalo Alice." **Alice,** which lies to the southwest of **Embden** and **Chaffee,** is near a gumbo slough that each spring and fall hosts vast numbers of migrating Canada geese. Other towns in Cass County include **Page** (329, **Davenport, Durbin, Erie, Ayr** (42) and **Absaraka,** named for the Absaroke Indians, the first known residents of the area, better known as Gros Ventres or Hidatsa.

Tower City (293) was named not for Gothic spires but for Charlemagne Tower, a director of the Northern Pacific Railroad. Tower City's fortunes briefly flourished during the 1880s along with plans to establish a Baptist college. It was to be named Tower University after its hoped-for benefactor. But fate stepped in after only two years when its attorney namesake declined to continue his support.

The Barnes County line lies just west of Tower City. The county, which marks the westernmost edge of ancient Lake Agassiz, was named for Judge Alanson Barnes, associate justice of Dakota Territory.

Unlike the dozens of towns christened in honor of real-life women, **Oriska** bears the distinction of being the only North Dakota city named after the heroine of a book, Lydia Sigourney's *Poems and Legends of the West.*

Valley City (7,774) was the fifth name suggested for the city which grew up where the Northern Pacific Railroad crossed the Sheyenne River. Earlier appellations included both Wahpeton and Worthington, which went on to caption other townsites.

Local sports teams draw their nickname, the Hi-Liners, from the mile-long Northern Pacific Railroad bridge, constructed in the first decade of the twentieth century, which crosses the valley at a height of nearly 150 feet. Despite its high profile, the bridge's connection to the prairie still requires steep grades. During the 1920s local pranksters took revenge on railroad yard detectives whom they deemed unduly harsh by greasing the rails with gallons of animal fat collected from local butchers. Trains arrived downhill in record time, but couldn't make the grade when trying to depart. The scheme worked even better than anticipated; the rails had to be scourged with burning brush to allow them to exit uphill.

Valley City State College was established by the state constitution to train teachers; its first classes were held in 1890. Among its most noted graduates is sculptor Paul Fjelde, a native of Hoople.

Since 1936 the city has hosted tens of thousands of visitors each March for the annual North Dakota Winter Show. Once described as a county fair in a deep freeze, the show revolves around livestock competitions, women's contests and events, big-name entertainment and a sanctioned professional indoor rodeo.

North of Valley City, the Sheyenne River backs up behind Bald Hill Dam to form **Lake**

The Northern Pacific High-Line bridge at Valley City.

Ashtabula, one of North Dakota's most picturesque lakes and a prime site for boating and fishing for walleye and northern pike. Several resorts and private cabins line its well-shaded shoreline, along with public campgrounds at Eggert's Landing and Mel Rieman Recreation Area.

Wildlife abounds in the area, including hundreds of pelicans who cruise the dam's tailrace to feast on addled fish dizzied by their trip through its turbines. The Federal Fish Hatchery nearby produces astronomical numbers of walleye fingerlings each year. Swans, giant Canada and snow geese, and other waterfowl make their home on its fish-rich rearing ponds.

The village of **Pillsbury** (46) lies just east of Sibley Crossing, the northernmost point of the lake. Here General William Hastings Sibley's forces crossed the Sheyenne in July 1863 in pursuit of Sioux bands believed to have participated in the bloody Minnesota Sioux uprising of 1862.

The Steele County Historical Society has restored several Main Street buildings in **Hope** (406) including the Little Red School House and Baldwin's Arcade, a boardwalk-fronted structure now on the National Register of Historic Places. The former clinic has been divided into period rooms depicting pioneer life.

South of Valley City along N.D. #32 are the cities of **Fingal** (151), **Lucca** and **Nome** (67).

West of the intersection of N.D. 32 and 46, the prairie suddenly breaks open into the deep valley of the Sheyenne River. At the bottom is **Little Yellowstone Park**, a cool and shady respite from the arrow-straight highway. The park offers an invitation to camp, picnic, play softball or hike along the mellow river's banks.

Take your choice: Wander north or south along a scenic drive. To the north is the little town of **Kathryn**. To its east, the log-cabin home of pioneer settler Carl Jensen and his nephew John Bjerklie, built in 1878, still stands at the margin of a field. The site of the Walker Flour Mill, one of the first on the Sheyenne, is just to the north.

To the south lies **Fort Ransom State Park**, one of North Dakota's newest. Carved out of the natural woodlands, it offers camping, hiking, picnic grounds and interpretive programs throughout the summer. The annual Sodbuster Days, held on the first weekend after the Fourth of July, recreate early homestead days and ways with horse-drawn plowing, threshing, buggy rides and more. Plans are underway to renovate two sites within the park — the century-old Sunne farm as a living history area, and the Bjone house as an interpretive center and park headquarters.

The site of **Fort Ransom** tops a hill several miles below the park. It was established in 1867 as the first of a chain of fortifications planned to keep prairie settlers safe from the Sioux. Its buildings were surrounded by a 12-foot wall of timber and sod, itself encircled by an eight-foot ditch...ultimately judged an over-reaction to the Indian threat, since few even passed through the area in those days. Signs abound of earlier residents, however, including Standing Rock, a boulder scored by four deep grooves which Indians believed were incised by spirits. It was noted in 1839 by explorers Nicollet and Fremont.

The village of **Fort Ransom** is nestled down below. Its Ransom County Historical Museum displays artifacts related to the pioneer era. The community attracts thousands of visitors for its Sheyenne Valley Arts & Crafts Festival in late September, drawing area crafters and antiquers along with farm enthusiasts for an old-time threshing bee. A fishing derby is held each summer. In winter skiing enthusiasts take advantage of one of the state's few slopes,

A wildlife refuge tucked between the valleys of the Sheyenne and James rivers shelters the continent's largest nesting colony of pelicans.

Fort Ransom State Park is the scene the first weekend following July Fourth each summer for Sodbuster Days. The two-day event recalls the era of farm work with teams of horses. Hay is cut and stacked in the barn of the Sunne Farm, land is plowed and crops are cut and readied for a steam thresher...all by horses and experienced hands. Many grandparents bring their grandchildren to Sodbuster Days to show them how life on the farm used to be.

16

with a tow lift carrying skiers to the top of a 1,000-foot run dropping 300 feet.

Several routes complete the circle of southeastern North Dakota. The first, turning eastward on N.D. #46, leads to **Enderlin** (1,161), early in its history the district headquarters for the Soo Line Railroad; a Soo locomotive is permanently sidelined in Patrick Pierce Park. Here National Sun Products refines low-cholesterol safflower oil from one of two varieties of sunflowers grown in fields throughout the region. The second variety, confectionery, is roasted and salted as a snack food under the brand name Dakota Kid and others.

Maple Creek Historic Site four miles north of **Leonard** (289) marks a crossing used as early as 1825 by Selkirk colonists traveling between Fort Garry and St. Paul, and in the 1840s by ox cart trains of fur traders. Others who passed here included Gov. Alexander Ramsey in 1851 en route to parley with the Chippewa, Gov. I.I. Stevens during his 1853 survey of routes for a transcontinental railway, the gold-seeking wagon trains of Captain James Fisk in 1861, and Gen. H.H. Sibley in 1863.

The Runck Chateau Ranch five miles south of Leonard offers a unique dining experience on Wednesday and Friday evenings throughout the summer. Members of the Lynn Runck family serve up a home-cooked picnic highlighted by beefsteak and barbecued ribs, followed by wagon rides in the surrounding Sand Hills.

Kindred (568) — "the town where kindness is a way of life" — is headquarters for Cass County Rural Electric Cooperative, one of the largest and most innovative RECs in the nation.

Highway 46 joins Interstate 29 near Hickson. Nearby is Oxbow Country Club. Its golf course, widely considered the most challenging in the area, was designed by Robert Trent Jones Jr.

Further south on Highway 32 is the Ransom County seat of **Lisbon** (2,283) — named for its founders' roots, not in Portugal but in Illinois and New York. Picnickers in Lisbon Park can often watch canoeists paddle by on the Sheyenne. Camping is available in Sandager Park and Dead Colt Creek Recreation Area five miles south of the city. Pioneer Lisbon newspaper publisher W.D. Boyce is credited with importing the concept for the Boy Scouts from England to the United States. The verdant campus of the North Dakota Veterans Home, established in 1891, provides pleasant retirement living for military vets. Other Ransom County towns include **Sheldon** (173), **Elliott** (44), **Englevale**, **McLeod** and **Anselm**.

Back on N.D. 32, **Gwinner** (725) welcomes you to Sargent County. The town is best known for the Melroe Company, a homegrown manufacturer of skid-steer loaders and other farm equipment. Now a division of Clark Equipment, its corporate headquarters are in Fargo and its Spra-Coupes are built in Bismarck, but Gwinner is still home. Like the loaders that gave the town its place in history, the high school basketball team is called the Bobcats.

Crete and **Stirum** lie to the west. Heading east on N.D. 13 carries you past **Milnor** (716) and **DeLamere** into Richland County and then **Wyndmere** (550). Its English-sounding name combines "wynd," a narrow land, with "mere," a pool — an apt description before the townsite was ditched and drained. Today's location is actually the site of East Wyndmere, established a mile east of the original some 15 years later. When the western town was abandoned, residents dropped the "east."

The rural area north of **Barney** (70) and Mooreton was among the first to be served by a consolidated school on the banks of Antelope Creek.

Bonanza farms dotted Richland County during the 1880s. Hugh Moore, owner of Antelope Farm, is the namesake of **Mooreton** (216).

Abandoned buildings of the F.A. Bagg farm, now on the National Register of Historic Places, are still standing south of town. Bagg's acreage was so farflung that during the '30s and '40s he maintained three airplanes to visit distant fields.

Back on N.D. 32, the route's southernmost leg leads through the Sargent County seat of **Forman** (629), located in the exact center of the county, and **Havana** (148), which stands less than one mile north of the South Dakota border. When Havana's aging town cafe finally closed its doors, the townspeople didn't take its loss lightly. They organized a community cooperative whose volunteers now operate it as a public service, taking turns as cooks and waiters. Despite evidence to the contrary (suggested by the proximity of another town of even more slender population dubbed Cuba), Havana is said to be named after a city in Illinois. Silver Lake five miles northeast of the city is the setting for Laura Ingall Wilder's book *By the Shore of Silver Lake*.

East of Forman on N.D. 11 lie **Rutland** (250) and **Cayuga** (75). The nearby Tewaukon National Wildlife Refuge is known for its dense population of small birds, waterfowl, pelicans, cormorants and sandhill cranes, as well as prairie animals. Its name is the Sioux word for "skunk." A trading post and dance pavilion once stood on its north shore. While Cayuga was named after a tribe of the Iroquois Confederation back east, its Dakota neighbors are the Sisseton Sioux, most of whose reservation lies in South Dakota.

Other Sargent County towns include **Crete**, **Stirum**, **Cogswell**, **Straubville**, **Brampton** and **Geneseo**.

Many Czechoslovakians settled near **Lidgerwood** (971). The local ZCBJ Lodge building (now owned by the Knights of Columbus) bears testimony to their influence along with a favorite local pastry, the jam-filled kolache.

The American mother house of the Sisters of St. Francis in **Hankinson** (1,158); the order

was founded in Germany in 1241. The convent is the home of Sister Rosalia Haberl, whose work earned her a Smithsonian Institutions folk art fellowship to preserve the art of bobbin lace, one she has practiced for 80 years. Just outside Hankinson, Lake Elsie provides a setting for swimming, boating, fishing and lakeside relaxation. In fall, the area's sand hills become a mecca for hunters of sandhill cranes and other game birds.

N.D. 11 approaches the Minnesota border at **Fairmount** (480). A landmark in the yard of St. Anthony's Catholic Church gained fame decades ago as the Sermon in Stone. Constructed of brightly colored stones and ores by a local priest, it symbolized the ten commandments, the virtues of faith, hope and charity, the trinity and the sacraments.

A sign at the point of entry from South Dakota on old U.S. 81 bears the gracious legend, "You are now leaving South Dakota and entering North Dakota — our twin state at creation, a great state of the land. Famous for its Red River Valley, wheat and a progressive and self-reliant people." A second marker notes, "You are about to enter Richland County, the southerly four miles of which was once in Roberts County (South Dakota), which you are leaving. It has a notable history, splendid terrain and a fine citizenry." To the west, the two states' border was marked at statehood by pink granite cairns positioned precisely every three-quarters mile — most still in place today.

Wahpeton (9,064), the county seat of Richland County, lies ten miles east of I-29 across the Red River from Breckenridge, Minn. A bridge between the two marks the spot where the Bois de Sioux and Ottertail Rivers collaborate to form the Red; their wooded banks suggest the meaning of the city's Indian name, "Village of the Leaves." Public boat launching facilities offer anglers a chance for walleye, northern pike or what's considered by some to be the river's finest delicacy, the catfish.

(Top left) Visitors today can still see the protective palisades of Fort Abercrombie, which helped make it an important post on the frontier, guarding commerce on the Red River.
(Left) Efforts are underway to preserve the historic Bagg Farm, the sole survivor of the bonanza farms which once flourished in the valley. (Above) One reason why Wahpeton is North Dakota's most industrial city is the State School of Science, which prepares students for today's highly technological job market.

18

The North Dakota College of Science has been a national model of industrial education since the early 1900s. Today its courses blend junior college, business school and vocational curricula, keeping pace with the times through the addition of areas relevant to modern technology. Generations of native American youth have attended the U.S. Indian School just west of the college campus.

Chahinkapa Park — "top of the trees" in Sioux — lies between the old shore of the Red River and its current course. Once Sioux bands camped here for their summer buffalo hunts. Today its RV camping and picnic facilities, softball fields and children's playground attract a host of families every summer weekend. Its biggest attraction, though, is the Chahinkapa Zoo, whose denizens range from bison, moose and bear to monkeys, songbirds and baby farm animals. Tame Canada geese, swans and ducks skim the surface of winding waterways, occasionally making noisy forays on land to demand tidbits from the picnic basket.

Next to the park, the Richland County Historical Museum displays memorabilia from the county's early years. Its exhibits include a noteworthy collection of Rosemeade Pottery, the brightly colored salt-and-pepper sets and knick knacks manufactured through the 1950s from native clay in a local factory. Among other local landmarks is a unique monument in a cemetery south of town — a marble tent pole erected by colleagues of a circus roustabout killed by lightning years ago.

A combination of ambitious local leadership and good location has made Wahpeton into North Dakota's most industrial city. Local manufacturing plants include Wil-Rich and Ro-Banks Manufacturing, the former specializing in farm equipment, the latter in high-quality machine tooled components. Wahpeton Canvas Company founder Edward Shorma was honored in 1982 as SBA and *Nation's Business* Magazine's small businessman of the year. Area farmers' sugarbeets are pro-

cessed at Minn-Dak Farmers Cooperative. A division of 3M for several years manufactured audio and video tapes in Wahpeton; its establishment sparked a protest led by rock star Bruce Springsteen when functions of an older New Jersey plant were transferred to the prairie. The Boss was nowhere to be heard, however, when that operation later pulled out of North Dakota.

North of Wahpeton on the parallel routes of Interstate 29 and U.S. 81 is the cloistered convent of the Sisters of Mary of Carmel, with its manicured grounds and serene setting, and the towns of **Dwight** (72) and **Galchutt**. Dwight bears the name of U.S. Congressman John Dwight of New York, who headed the Dwight Farm and Land Company in Richland and Steele Counties. One of his stockholders (and later the firm's president) was John Miller, North Dakota's first governor, who went on to found a grain commission firm in Duluth.

Abercrombie (260) is situated west of the reconstructed blockhouses and stockade of Fort Abercrombie, the first military reservation constructed in North Dakota. Dating from 1858, it saw action during the Minnesota Sioux Uprising of 1862, when settlers flocked inside its stockade for safety from attacking Indians. It played an important part in early North Dakota history — as a way station on the Red River ox cart trail, as a stop along the way for Montana-bound wagon trains of gold-seekers and for Dakota-bound homesteaders, as the launching point for the *Anson Northrup*, first steamboat on the Red River, and as the scene of the signing of a peace treaty with Sioux and Chippewa bands which ended their harassment of settlers in eastern North Dakota. The Fort Abercrombie Historical Museum displays relics of the Indian wars and settlement period.

Highway 81 reenters Cass County after passing **Colfax** (101), **Walcott** (186) and **Christine** (147), a village named for Swedish opera soprano Christine Nilsson. Other

Richland County towns include **Mantador** (76) and **Great Bend** (113). The town of **Wild Rice** on the banks of the river with the same name is one of North Dakota's oldest, settled by French-Canadians in the 1860s. The first resident of its old cemetery is said to have been a priest beheaded by Indians in 1862.

A gaggle of new small towns has sprung up around Fargo, including **Briarwood, Prairie Rose, Frontier** and (north of the city) **Reile's Acres.** All are basically bedroom communities for Fargo-Moorhead. **Horace** (494) shares that role, but dates back to 1875, when the first post office was christened in honor of newspaperman Horace Greeley, whose voice still rings out over the prairie after a century of ups and downs, great victories and silent defeats: "Go west, young man, and grow up with the country." III

Viewed from the air, the Red River Valley is a fertile carpet of green, broken only by the meandering and heavily wooden river. Farms and fields are usually set out in precise, straight lines.

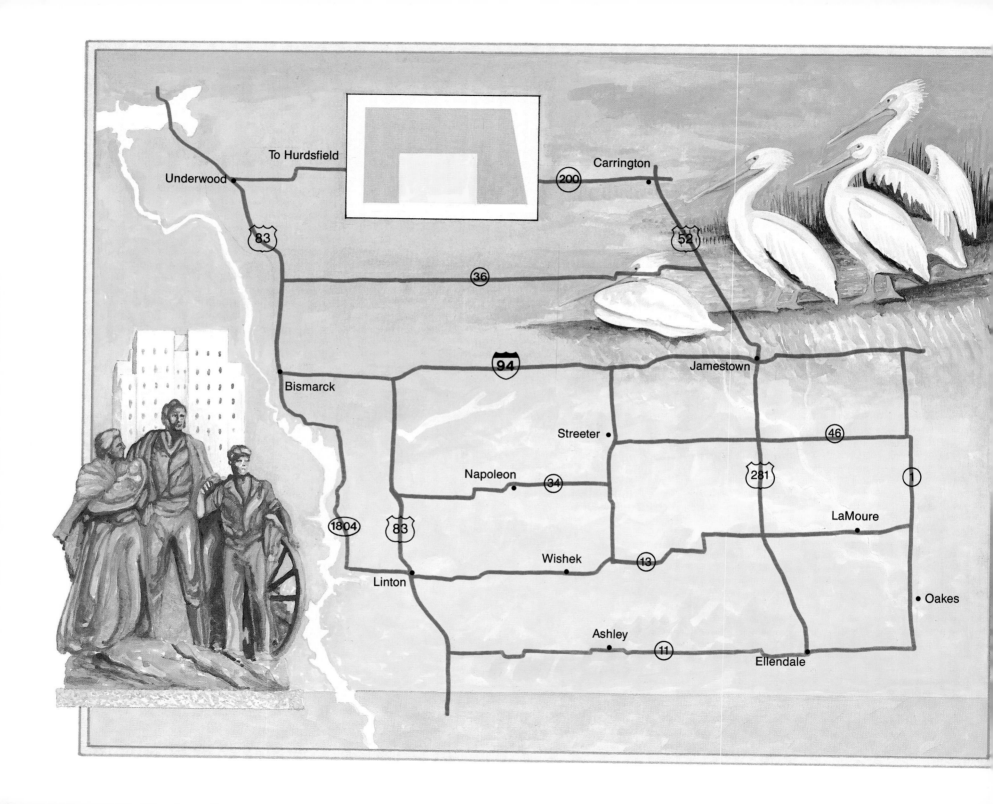

Prairie Pothole Country

The Highlights: The Coteau du Missouri — hills marking the farthest advance of Ice Age glaciers — are cloaked in prairie lands once black with American bison, and now shadowed by the wings of North American birds and waterfowl which nest and breed in pothole country. Here the U.S. Army clashed with bands of Sioux, and wagon trains carried the first generation of white Dakotans to their homesteads, and Germans from Russia established dynasties in a land that resembled the steppes they'd left behind.

The Route: Beginning in Bismarck, follow Interstate 94 east to past Steele, Tappen and Medina to Jamestown and, a few miles further on, the junction with N.D. Highway 1. At this point, you may choose one of two routes. Turn south toward LaMoure, Oakes and Ellendale; choose westward routes N.D. 13 or N.D. 11 (with N.D. 46 as an alternate), and then close the loop with a return to Bismarck via U.S. Highway 83. Or go north on N.D. 1, turning west at Cooperstown onto N.D. 200 (with several choices of side trips), joining U.S. 83 at Underwood for the final leg of the tour.

Welcome to **Bismarck**. North Dakota's capital, with a 1980 population of 44,485, has been the scene of turbulent political battles since even before statehood, when operatives of the Northern Pacific Railroad snatched the territorial capital away from Yankton, South Dakota.

Several settlements grew into the city, which traces its beginning to Camp Greeley (named for Horace "Go west young man" Greeley) and later Hancock, a military encampment set up across from Fort Abraham Lincoln (then McKeen) to defend Northern Pacific Railroad construction crews from the Sioux Indians. When the railroad arrived in 1872, it named the civilian encampment Bismarck in honor of Germany's Iron Chancellor, and in hopes of thus attracting German capital and settlers. Camp Hancock Historic Site downtown preserves the Army's log headquarters as well as Bread of Life Episcopal Church, the city's first, and an NP steam locomotive.

The State Capitol rises 19 stories above the city. Its modern lines and art deco touches are the legacy of the Dirty '30s, when the original red brick territorial capitol burned down. It was designed by Joseph Bell DeRemer of Grand Forks and William F. Kurke of Fargo in association with Holabird and Root of Chicago; legend has it that its design was originally developed for a Windy City skyscraper project derailed by the Depression. The cornerstone was laid on Sept. 4, 1933, the 50th anniversary of the dedication of the original building. The handsome Great Hall includes tall windows, fluted bronze pillars, walls and floors of travertine and marble, and elevator doors decorated with a frieze of heroic figures.

The North Dakota Heritage Center houses the State Historical Society's offices and collections, as well as a vast and fascinating interpretive museum thoroughly exploring the region's history, economy and people. The Glass Box Gift Shop stocks a selection of North Dakota books, jewelry, gifts and toys.

Also located on the Capitol grounds are the Liberty Memorial Building, which houses the State Library; the Highway Building; an arboretum of trees and shrubs, and the contemporary ranch-style home of the governor. The original Victorian-style Governor's Mansion, restored to its charming traditional 1884 splendor, is open for tours throughout the summer; it's located near downtown.

General Sibley Park south of the city was once known as Burnt Boat Island, memorializing a tale of gold miners returning from Fort Benton who ran afoul of Indians. They were killed in the melee and their boat burned. The fortune in gold which they were said to be carrying was never recovered. "Island" was originally an accurate description until the powerful Missouri changed its course and left it high and dry. The modern name honors Gen. Henry Hastings Sibley, who in 1863 led an Army force west in reprisal for the Minnesota Sioux Uprising of 1862; historic sites related to that campaign and the parallel contingent led by Gen. Alfred Sully are frequent throughout south central North Dakota.

A modern riverboat named after the *Far West*, a paddlewheel

North Dakota's well-planned and spacious Capitol Grounds hosts a variety of activities throughout the year...from concerts, arts weekends, walking tours and cross-country ski lessons, to soccer matches during the Prairie Rose State Games.

steamboat that plied the Missouri during the days of the war between the U.S. Army and the Indians, now rides the river from its Bismarck port. Visitors also enjoy the Dakota Zoo, with some 125 species of mostly-native birds and animals, and kiddie rides just outside the entrance in Riverside Park. Local and regional artists' creations are displayed at the Elan Gallery, once the home of the late poet laureate James Foley, author of the "North Dakota Hymn" as well as 22 volumes of poetry.

Along with the Capitol, Bismarck boasts the State Penitentiary (chosen by local delegates during the horse-trading of state institutions which surrounded the state constitutional convention) and Bismarck State College, a two-year junior college and vocational school. The state-owned Bank of North Dakota stands as evidence of the Nonpartisan League's populist program to throw off the bonds of Minneapolis' economic imperialism during the 'teens and '20s. It remains the only financial institution under a state's ownership in the United States.

The University of Mary is sponsored by the Benedictine Sisters, whose Annunciation Priory shares the bluff above Apple Creek south of the city. College and convent were designed by architect Marcel Breuer. Their sturdy lines are shaped in ageless native stone and stern concrete, creating an aesthetic impression of permanence and stability.

The United Tribes Educational Technical Center now occupies the former Fort Lincoln south of the city. Not to be confused with Fort Abraham Lincoln across the river, this post was established by Congress in 1896, occupied in 1903, and ultimately decommissioned in 1913. During World War II the federal government used it as an internment camp for captured German soldiers. Now United Tribes draws dancers and musicians from throughout the plains to its annual pow wow — one of the nation's largest — in September.

One of the biggest and most colorful events in the Northern Plains is the annual United Tribes International Pow Wow, held each September.

Eastbound out of Bismarck, Interstate 94 crosses through Burleigh County (named for Dr. Walter A. Burleigh, Indian agent at Yankton and Dakota Territory delegate to Congress). Its first stop is **Menoken**, whose Indian name is said to mean "Thou shalt reap what thou hast sown." The archeological remains of an 18th century Mandan Indian village. Dish-like depressions where earth lodges stood are surrounded by a large dry moat and four clearly defined bastions are preserved at Menoken Historical Site. Historians believe that it was here Pierre de la Verendrye, the first white explorer documented in North Dakota, met with representatives of the tribe in 1738.

The small town of **McKenzie** is one of three North Dakota entities named for famed railroad boss Alexander McKenzie. (The others are McKenzie County and the town of Alexander.) The settlers who founded **Sterling**, next in line, named it for their Illinois hometown. As for **Driscoll**, it was named for newspaper editor Frederick Driscoll of the *St. Paul Pioneer Press*, considered the official house organ of the Northern Pacific Railroad.

Chaska Historic Site north of Driscoll marks the spot where General Sibley's expedition buried one of his Indian scouts in 1863. South of town is Long Lake, surrounded by Long Lake National Wildlife Refuge.

Steele (796), the Kidder County seat, was chartered by the territorial legislature in 1882; at the time it claimed to be the smallest city in the United States. That flair for publicity reflects the bombast of Col. Wilbur F. Steele, who arrived from New York to become the county's first settler in 1877. In an even more flamboyant gesture, he sent the first North Dakota State Legislature a certified check for $100,000, to be cashed if they

Each December, lights from the tower offices are shaped and colored to resemble a Christmas tree...and on New Year's Eve, the numbers of the new year are displayed on the state's skyscraper Capitol Building. (Right) A symphony concert on the Heritage Center plaza.

acceded to his request to relocate the capitol to his namesake. Steele built his own railroad, the Steele-Alaska Northwestern, a grand-sounding enterprise that was actually a half-mile spur from the NP line to his brick plant northeast of town. Challenged by the directors of more substantial railways, he countered, "While my line may not be as long as yours, I want it understood that it's every bit as wide."

South of **Dawson** (144) is Lake Isabel, the site of Camp Grassick. This camp was founded by the North Dakota Anti-Tuberculosis Association and named for a pioneer Grand Forks physician. The Elks acquired it in 1947 and operate it as a summer camp for children with disabilities.

Slade National Wildlife Refuge encompasses the lodge and game preserve of James J. Hill's son-in-law G.L. Slade, who raised pheasants and ducks on a lake he created himself by pumping water from wells. The refuge is now operated by the U.S. Fish and Wildlife Service.

In 1878 **Tappen** (271) was known as Troy Farm Siding after the Troy Farm, a bonanza enterprise of more than 10,000 acres operated by S. Tappen and John Van Dusen, both from Troy, New York. McPhail's Butte Historic Site seven miles north of the town marks the location of the Battle of Big Mound, one of three encounters between Gen. Henry Hastings Sibley's troops and Sioux Indians during the campaign of 1863. It's named in honor of Col. Samuel McPhail, commander of the Minnesota Rangers. The Army contingent met the same Indians the next day at Dead Buffalo Lake and again four days later at Stony Lake.

The Sibley expedition camped at **Crystal Springs**, naming it for the source of the waters of Crystal Springs Lake.

The name of **Medina** (521) may have been derived from "median," or midpoint, since the Northern Pacific Railroad considered it midway between the extreme eastern coast of United States and the westernmost shore of

Alaska. Then again, it might have been the city of Medina, New York. In the beginning residents and visitors alike called it "Med-EE-na." In 1949, however, its citizens changed the pronunciation to "Med-EYE-na" in honor of Judge Harold Medina, who presided over the trial and conviction of 11 members of the Communist Party. He visited Medina in August 1956 when the name change was made official.

Chase Lake National Wildlife Refuge ten miles north of Medina is best known as the larger of only two pelican breeding colonies in North America. Ten thousand pelicans, along with cormorants and gulls, hatch eggs and raise their young on two islands far from the predators on shore. Fish cannot survive in its highly alkaline waters.

The waters of Lake George, on the other hand, support a healthy population of tiny brine shrimp. Otherwise known as Salt Lake,

it is located seven miles northwest of **Streeter** (264). It's said to be the deepest natural lake (at 128 feet) in North Dakota. On its south shore, Streeter Memorial Park — dedicated to the memory of World War I veterans — offers a swimming beach and picnic facilities. The town itself dates from 1904. Three sources are offered for its name: Col. Darwin Streeter, prominent legislator from Emmons County which, like the Streeter area, was settled by Germans from Russia; J.B. Streeter, the townsite owner, developer and farmer; or Streater, Ill., former home of the president of the townsite company which developed the town.

No such debate clouds the origins of **Cleveland** (130), the next town east on I-94. Its original settlers came from Ohio. Neighboring **Windsor** was named for the city in Ontario. Here a relatively steep rise (in plains terms) of 300 feet marks division

between the Central Lowlands and Great Plains. It's a full-fledged continental divide, though somewhat less dramatic than the east-west division in the Rocky Mountains; here waters part ways in the other direction, flowing south to Gulf of Mexico or north to Hudson's Bay. Just on the other side is **Eldridge**, honoring Iowa investor D.T. Eldridge, who developed a large farm in the area.

Like Bismarck, **Jamestown** (16,280) was sired by the Northern Pacific Railway and the U.S. Army, which assigned troops to protect construction crews. Railroad engineers were the settlement's first residents in 1871, joined the next spring by soldiers from Fort Ransom. A few months later, Fort Seward was built on a hill overlooking the James River, named in honor of William Seward, Abraham Lincoln's secretary of state. Strategically planted in the middle of northern Dakota Territory, it became an important supply depot for forts further west as well as a stop along mailriders' trans-Dakota routes.

Today the Fort Seward Historical Society operates an interpretive center next to the state-owned historical site. Each summer wagon trains carry modern adventurers across the prairie, winding up with a final encampment on the old fort's grounds. A county historical group operates the Stutsman County Memorial Museum in a handsome old brick residence not far from downtown.

Jamestown had been an avid contender for the territorial capitol in 1883, when Bismarck ultimately snatched it from Yankton, S.D. After the capital building burned in 1930, boosters saw a second chance. Once again they mounted a campaign based on their city's more central location; but voters doused the dreams of both Jamestown and an even darker dark-horse candidate, New Rockford.

The highest profile attraction in Jamestown is the 60-ton concrete buffalo that stands guard just north of Interstate 94. Frontier Village at his feet includes a variety of old-time buildings including a blockhouse, school,

North Dakota's prairie pothole country is a prime breeding ground for for many species of birds and waterfowl.

24

Little remains of the wagon trains and trails which hauled the pioneers to the prairies of Dakota...except the spirit of the people who refuse to let the past die. Each summer the Fort Seward Wagon Train sets out over the central North Dakota sod, recreating pioneer days of travel by wagon and dinners cooked over an open fire.

railroad depot and gallery displaying the works of the late western artist James Kirkpatrick. Local musicians and actors stage the Frontier Follies each summer in a natural outdoor amphitheater.

Jamestown is the home of two educational institutions, the Anne Carlsen School and Jamestown College, founded in 1883 by the Presbyterian Church. The former, owned by Lutheran Health Systems of Fargo, is a residential school for physically and mentally handicapped young people from kindergarten through high school. Retired longtime director Carlsen has been honored throughout the country for her leadership in promoting dignity and independence for the disabled.

Besides Carlsen, Jamestown has been the home of two other members of North Dakota's Rough Rider Hall of Fame — western writer Louis L'Amour, the best-selling author of all time, and jazz singer Peggy Lee. Famed playwright Maxwell Anderson also attended school here.

Incongruous though it may seem on the windswept prairie, the Jamestown area is one of mid-Dakota's major water playgrounds. Northwest of town is the Pipestem Dam, whose long, skinny reservoir has yielded respectable-sized walleyes. Directly north of the city is Jamestown Dam and its chain of large, very shallow lakes, Jim, Maud and Arrowwood. Campsites and boat rentals are available at Lakeside Marina and Smokey's Landing along with other services and supplies.

Arrowwood National Wildlife Refuge surrounds the northernmost sections of the manmade lakes, supporting a heavy summer population of shore birds, ducks and geese. Several driving trails initiate visitors into this segment of the so-called North American waterfowl factory.

At Jamestown a choice must be made: Whether to travel east on I-94 to its junction

Due to its central location, the Chieftain Lodge in Carrington regularly hosts state-wide meetings and conferences, and is a popular rest stop for travelers.

with N.D. Highway 1, and then south and west; or to take U.S. 281 north of town to N.D. 200.

North Loop: The northern route along U.S. 281 leads first to **Pingree**, and thereby hangs a tale. The area's original homesteader was Hazen Senter Pingree, who arrived in 1880 with a hayrack, wagon and oxen team determined to start a potato plantation. When that enterprise failed, he went to Detroit and, starting out as a shoe manufacturer, went on to become the city's mayor and a two-term governor of Michigan. The early landowner for whom the community was actually named, David Pingree, was from Salem, Mass.

Other Stutsman County towns include **Kensal** (210), named for a resort town in County Cork, Ireland; Oswego, after a New York town; **Edmunds**, named by a pair of twin pioneer

physicians for their friend, the U.S. senator from Vermont; and **Courtenay** (110) with its English derivation.

One westward option is N.D. Highway 36 past **Woodworth**, **Pettibone**, **Lake Williams**, **Robinson** (named for the president of a Steele bank), **Tuttle**, **Arena**, **Wing** and **Regan**. These towns are among the youngest in the state, dated from the 'teens. Like most settlements that have survived through the state centennial, they emerged following the arrival of the railroad — in their cases, secondary branch lines built inland from the main routes.

Continuing north on U.S. 281 are **Melville** and **Carrington**, both named for one Melville Carrington of the Carrington and Casey Land Company that developed the area. The company, which also operated a bonanza farm south of the city of Carrington, donating town lots for the Foster County Courthouse, park, school and churches.

Carrington (2,641) is headquarters for the Garrison Diversion Conservancy District. The project was authorized in 1944 as part of the Pick-Sloan Missouri Basin program to shepherd development of a massive system of open canals intended to carry Missouri River water to the dry farmlands of central North Dakota...a payback for the estimated $4.5 billion in losses the state incurred through the Garrison and Oahe Dams. Embattled by U.S. and Canadian environmentalists and federal budget balancers, the project hangs on today by the skin of its teeth. Irrigated acreage has been trimmed back from a projected million acres in 1944 to just 130,000. The only canal to be completed can be seen in the McClusky area. North Dakota State University operates an Irrigation Branch Station at Carrington as well as a Livestock Experiment Station.

North Dakota's first real motel, the Rainbow Gardens, was built here in 1930 by Japanese immigrant Harry Hayashi. Twenty-eight brightly colored cabins surrounded a careful garden complete with goldfish and li-

A much smaller Garrison Diversion project than the grand irrigation plan once envisioned has canals winding through central North Dakota in search of thirsty land.

ly pond, a miniature waterfall, children's wading pool and playground. After the onset of anti-Japanese sentiment at the beginning of World War II, Hayashi was taken into custody by the government and held at Fort Lincoln south of Bismarck. After his release he attempted to renovate the motel, which had badly deteriorated, but eventually was forced to sell it. It burned down in 1953.

Carrington is still known for a motel, however — the Chieftain, with its 30-foot Indian statue and hallway displays of authentic Indian artifacts and antique guns. Not far away the Foster County Historical Society maintains a local museum that's open on Sunday afternoons.

U.S. Highway 52 and N.D. 200 speed travelers west from Carrington past the turnoff for **Cathay** (said to have been named by

a Chinese cook for the Soo Line construction crew), **Sykeston** (193), **Heaton, Bowdon** (220), **Chasely** and **Hurdsfield** (113). A reminder of the glory foretold by eager land merchants is the Hurd Round House topping a hill southwest of Hurdsfield. The house, rectangular at its foot but topped by a circular second story, was built in 1900 by Northern Pacific land agent Warren Hurd to entertain prospective buyers. After years of disuse the Wells County Historical Society acquired the property and has worked toward its restoration. It was entered on the National Register of Historic Places in 1977.

The Sheridan County towns of **Goodrich** (288), **Denhoff** and the county seat, **McClusky** (658), owe their starts at the turn of the century to the Northern Pacific's arrival. The McClusky Canal snakes through the area bearing a fraction of the Missouri River's flow. The area was the site during the early 1970s of the first bitter protests organized by the self-designated Committee to Save North Dakota, a group of environmentalists and affected landowners opposed to Garrison Diversion.

Mercer (134) bears the name of a Civil War veteran from Pennsylvania who first settled

The city of Turtle Lake calls itself the gateway to the lake district, a reference to the many lakes formed by glaciers retreating from central North Dakota millions of years ago. Strawberry Lake and Brush Lake are popular recreation sites.

at Painted Woods in 1869, raising the first wheat crop north of Bismarck. He ranched near here during the 1880s. Mercer County, also named after him, is directly across the Missouri from his original Painted Woods farm.

The John E. Williams Memorial Nature Preserve northeast of **Turtle Lake** (802) has been nicknamed "Valley of the Moon" for its weirdly barren landscape now owned and managed by the Nature Conservancy. Broad windswept alkali lakes are surrounded by bleached salt-encrusted beaches strewn with glacial rocks. Yet it is full of life, from hardy salt grass and other prairie varieties to salt-tolerant crustaceans, shorebirds and waterfowl. Among the scarce species of long-legged birds are piping plovers, marbled godwits, phalaropes and cranes.

N.D. Highway 200 meets U.S. 83 at **Underwood** (1,329) on the eastern margin of North Dakota's lignite country. Unlike most smaller North Dakota towns, those of McLean, Mercer, Oliver and Dunn Counties grew rapidly through the 1970s with the development of mine-mouth power plants. Electricity generated by those plants crosses the prairie with a phalanx of highboy towers and transmission lines headed for the bright lights and electric toothbrushes of the Twin Cities.

The McLean County seat of **Washburn** (1,767) was named for Colden Washburn, governor of Wisconsin in 1872-74 whose brother W.D. Washburn founded the neighboring town of Wilton. Washburn was an important steamboat landing in pioneer times. The *Sioux* ferry in Riverside Park preserves a bit of the homestead era, while other reminders of area history are on display in the McLean County Historical Museum.

Lewis and Clark spent the winter of 1804-1805 near Washburn in a stockade they called Fort Mandan. Today the fort — including a reconstructed log stockade and trading post — is maintained by the McLean

Rekindling visions of the Corps of Discovery, these modern-day fur trappers pose outside reconstructed Fort Mandan, the winter home of Lewis & Clark in 1804-05.

County Historical Society. A state historic site ten miles to the west of the replica fort was originally thought to be the site of the encampment. It was here that the explorers met the teen-age girl who was to be their guide to the Pacific Ocean, Sakakawea. The Hidatsa village in which she lived west of the river is now part of the Knife River National Historic Site.

The river road dubbed N.D. 1804 heads south from Washburn, paralleling the river. It passes the mouth of Painted Woods Creek, where legend locates the doomed romance between a Mandan girl and Yanktonai Sioux boy, both killed by critics of their union. Their bodies were placed in the branches of a cottonwood tree whose bark peeled away, leaving a white and bony trunk. Local Sioux bands were said to have readied for battle in this grove, painting their faces and incidentally painting their threats on the trees in an early precursor of graffiti. Their subtle enemies the Mandans then splashed paint on surrounding trees to mock them. The entire thicket was destroyed by fire in 1951.

To the east on U.S. 83, **Wilton** (950) was the site of one of North Dakota's first lignite coal mines. W.D. Washburn opened Washburn Lignite Coal Mines and extended his Bismarck, Washburn & Great Falls Railroad (now the Soo Line) to Washburn to carry his coal in 1901. The Soo depot is maintained by the local historical society along with the intriguingly named Dingaling Museum.

Because of the many dams built to harness its destructive rampages, very little of the free-flowing Missouri River remains today. This stretch from Garrison Dam south to Bismarck still resembles the once great river, and looks much the way it did when the Big Muddy was the highway into the vast and unchartered frontier.

Just north of Bismarck is the Double Ditch Historical Site, where Mandan Indians lived 200 years ago in the large and prosperous Yellow Clay Village. Sunken rings throughout the area mark the foundations of their earth lodges. The town was surrounded by an earthen wall, a log palisade and an enormous dry moat 15 feet wide and nine feet deep.

By continuing east of Jamestown along Interstate 94 to the junction with N.D. Highway 1, travelers pass the town of **Spiritwood**. The name has special significance for the area northeast of Jamestown. The town draws its name from Spiritwood Farm, once the area's largest bonanza farm. The farm in turn is named after Spiritwood Lake, a long-time summer recreation area flanked by cabins and a venerable dance pavilion as well as a state fish hatchery. Anglers know it best as a source of occasional lunker walleyes and perch. The state's record muskie, a 24-pound specimen, was reeled in here during 1976.

The lake was known to Sioux as Minneskaya, or "water with foam on top." The English variant is based on another legend of star-crossed lovers. The Indian girl Minnewawa fell in love with a young man from another tribe; their relatives disapproved. When her lover was killed in battle with her own people on the opposite side of the lake, Minnewawa plunged into its waters to join him. Their spirits are said to linger in the area.

Past **Eckelson** and **Sanborn** (237) is the junction with N.D. Highway 1...like many major North Dakota roads, truly unswerving in its adherence to the straight and narrow.

Near its junction with N.D. 46 is Clausen Springs, a shady dimple of smooth waters and leafy grounds tucked below the horizon of the prairie. The park encompasses a small lake alive with rainbow trout, walleyes, largemouth bass and bullheads. Camping sites are available.

One of several westbound options, N.D. 46, lies south of the hamlet of **Hastings**. The road winds past the towns of **Litchville** (251), **Marion** (214), **Adrian, Millarton, Nortonville, Jud** (118) and **Alfred**. Alfred was established by a titled Englishman, Richard Sykes, who sold real estate and ranched in the vicinity, at one time owning 4,500 acres throughout LaMoure and adjoining counties. He named the city for Britain's great King Alfred and laid out streets with names like Winchester, Warwick and Avon.

Gackle (456), on the other hand, was named for a man who began as a humble shopkeeper. George Gackle arrived in the area in 1903; along with a partner, he established a country store south of the present town. A year later, when the Northern Pacific passed by eight miles to the north, the partners staked out a townsite and moved north to cash in on it. The enterprising Gackle later farmed nearly 11 sections of land, operated a number of huge grain elevators and sold furniture, hardware and farm implements throughout the area.

A jog south on N.D. 30 and 20 miles west on N.D. 34 carries visitors to **Napoleon**. Like Wishek and Ashley to the south, the city owes its beginnings to the arrival of the Minneapolis, St. Paul and Sault St. Marie Railroad in 1887 en route from Aberdeen and Eureka, S.D., to Bismarck. The railroad's marketing program in south Russia was critical to the area's settlement by German-Russian colonists. It was named for Napoleon Goodsill, president of the townsite company which cashed in on this fortunate state of affairs. Its first post office was two pigeonholes in a desk at the back of a general store.

Here The Judge's Chambers offers homemade lunches six days a week in the home of former Judge George McKenna. The house, including the dining area, is completely furnished with antiques. The furnishings are for sale, along with a selection of unusual gifts and a variety of sauce mixes and fresh pasta. Guests are frequently ferried from Bismarck via the Top Hat Limousine Service.

Distinctive, handcrafted iron crosses were popular with this region's German settlers who immigrated from Russia in the early 1900s.

A local historical museum displays other relics of Napoleon's past.

Burnstad, to the south, was named in 1907 for Christ Burnstad, the Logan County Cattle King, once grazed 50,000 head on 54 sections of land. Beaver Lake State Park offers an opportunity to cool off with a swim or fish for northern pike, perch and bullheads. Its grounds, like so many of the state's public works, bear testimony to the Works Progress Administration of the 1930s, which gave both desperately needed jobs and long-lived park and civic facilities to North Dakota.

Past **Kintyre** (the name of a Scottish peninsula in Irish Sea, home of the pioneer Campbell brothers who operated the Northwestern Livestock Company in the area) and **Brad-**

dock (86), N.D. 34 joins U.S. 83 at **Hazelton** (266). Once the self-appointed "Flax Capital of America," the city was known during the 1920s and '30s for its profusion of windmills...the legacy of a very successful traveling salesman.

Twenty miles south of the Highway 46 corner on N.D. Highway 1, its junction with N.D. 13 at **Verona** (126) offers an alternate route across the south central region. Like the nearby village of Grand Rapids, Verona was named after a city in Michigan.

LaMoure (1,077) and the county it serves were both named for Judson LaMoure, pioneer businessman and member of both the territorial and first state legislatures (as was the city of Jud). A decommissioned Minuteman missile stands beside the highway through town as part of a memorial honoring "Mr. Wheat," the late U.S. Senator Milton Young. One of his contributions to its welfare is Omega Station, the only U.S. Coast Guard tracking facility in North America. The major body of water hereabouts is Lake LaMoure, an impoundment on Cottonwood Creek popular among swimmers, picnickers and fishermen who favor rainbow trout and walleye. The *Red Wing*, a reconstruction of a paddlewheeler that once plied the nearby James River, stands high and dry west of the city limits.

LaMoure is a mecca for other enthusiasts, too — collectors of farm toys. The bible of that burgeoning hobby, *The Toy Farmer Magazine*, is published locally by Claire and Cathy Scheibe. The city hosts the annual North Dakota farm toy show in June.

LaMoure County Memorial Park is located a few miles north at **Grand Rapids**. The city — near a gurgling rapids on the James River — was the first to be established in the county and was named county seat in 1881. Five years later lost to LaMoure in the heated election of 1886. Displays in the LaMoure County Historical Museum — once the county courthouse — recount that violent era, along with more peaceable episodes. The LaMoure County Summer Theatre, an enthusiastic amateur group, produces several plays and musicals each year in the park pavilion.

Kulm (570) is the home town of actress Angie Dickinson, whose parents published the weekly *Kulm Messenger*. Like **Berlin** (57), its name honors the native land of area settlers: In this case, families from Kulms in both Germany and Russia.

Its founder's British birthplace inspired the name of **Edgeley** (843), the town which grew up at the highly favored junction of three railroads — the Northern Pacific and Milwaukee branch lines plus the main line of Midland Railway. The local Jackson Manufacturing Company manufactures ultralight aircraft which resemble a smaller version of the Piper J-3 Cub, popular among hobby pilots as well as farmers and ranchers who use them to look over their crops and livestock.

Both **Fredonia** (82) and **Lehr** (254) testify to the German-Russian roots of south central North Dakota. Until 1904 the former was called Denevitz, also a town is Bessarabia, Russia; a railroad official replaced it in 1904 with a word meaning "peace." Lehr, which is located in both Logan and McIntosh Counties, was one of the earliest towns established in North Dakota by German-Russians. It's named for the townsite owners,who led a colony of 50 settlers north from Eureka, S.D., via the Soo main line in 1886.

Wishek (1,345) was named for John R. Wishek Sr. of Ashley, who owned the townsite along the Soo Line route, and who donated land for the community's churches, parks, town hall and bandstand. Doyle Memorial State Park on the shore of Green Lake just south of town is a popular summer recreation spot.

A typical German-Russian sod house survives along N.D. 13 some 10 miles west of the city. This local style, like the log cabins of wooded areas, uses the most abundant local material — unimproved prairie sod — to fashion a sturdy home both cool in summer and warm in winter. Many traditional soddies extended directly into stables for housing livestock during the bitterly cold months.

The highway joins U.S. 83 at **Linton** (1,561), the county seat of Emmons County, whose name is taken from Missouri River steamboat captain James A. Emmons. Linton in turn was named for early attorney George Lynn (Lynn-Town). Area rancher Leo Kuntz maintains a herd of wild horses of the breed known as the American Horse. The animals are believed to be descended from stock ridden by Sitting Bull's warriors at the Little Big Horn; he acquired them from the National Park Service herd at Theodore Roosevelt National Park.

Original carvings above the courthouse windows depict the county's history. Nearby, the former Big Beaver Creek has become a bay renowned for as a fishing hot spot, thanks to backed up waters of Lake Oahe (impounded by the Missouri River dam at Pierre, S.D.).

Back on the final southbound stretch of N.D. Highway 1, the last town of size is **Oakes** (2,112). Though it was named for Thomas Oakes, an official of the Northern Pacific Railroad, its moniker also is rooted in a play on words: its major streets all bear the names of trees. The Dickey County Historical Society has created a pioneer village and museum

Growing in popularity, collectors of toy tractors and farm equipment gather each summer in LaMoure to complete their collections and discuss their hobby.

31

A monument to the German-Russians who settled this rocky landscape is this sod house, sitting defiantly along Highway 13 between Linton and Wishek.

here, complete with a one-room school, a century-old church and a railroad depot — a reminder of the importance of three railroads (the Northern Pacific, North Western and Soo Line) to the city's history.

Here the countryside offers clues to the geological past. This is the northern end of glacial Lake Dakota, a contemporary of better-known Lake Agassiz. The hills of the Missouri Plateau poke up against the horizon. The James River reigns, broad and powerful, carrying its waters toward the Gulf of Mexico. Here much research has been conducted on the agricultural potential and environment effects of the Garrison Diversion Project.

Five miles to the south, **Riverdale** — now a virtual ghost town — provides pleasant camping facilities.

N.D. Highway 11 works its way west through **Ludden** and **Guelph.** Though sedate today, the latter made history between 1883 and 1887 with an average of one and one-half name changes per year; they included Menasha Center (for a town in Wisconsin), Center, Centropolis, Centralia, Coldwater and Thatcherville (for a family among the original colony). Finally in 1889 it received its eighth and final designation for either Guelph, Ontario, birthplace of the Great Northern's James J. Hill, or Manfried Von Guelph, son of Duke Karl Otto of the princely Guelph family of Hanover, Germany. Rejected by his aristocratic family, he emigrated to America and passed through Dakota Territory; he's said to have run a local hardware store for a several years before moving on.

Dickey County's oldest city, **Ellendale** (1,967) dates from 1881, when officials of the Chicago, Milwaukee and St. Paul Railway christened it in honor of Mary Ellen Dale Merrill, wife of the railroad's superintendent. The community thrived as a result of the

The prairie pothole country can be a solitary experience on winding roads past small towns and pasture land.

The memorial to fallen soldiers at Whitestone Hill.

33

railroad's land advertisements in the Ukraine; the campaign drew tens of thousands of Germans from Russia to the Dakotas. As a result, Ellendale became a major supply point for the immigrant families on the eastern side of the so-called German-Russian Triangle of central North Dakota and north central South Dakota.

Trinity Bible College now occupies former campus of Ellendale Industrial and Teachers College, which in 1889 offered the United States' first free vocational training course. The state school was closed after its main facilities burned down 20 years ago. Today the private religious college is headquarters for the Lowell Lundstrom evangelical organization.

Monango (59), 10 miles north on U.S. Highway 281, may have been named after a wounded Indian child found strapped to a travois on the Whitestone Battlefield in 1863. Or an Indian chief? Or an official of the Milwaukee Railroad? Or an acronym composed of the first letter of each name submitted to Soo Line in a contest to christen the city? Some doubt remains. One point on which the pundits do agree is that a father and son from Kentucky, Beriah and Ebenezer Magoffin, were the first to arrive in 1884.

Some 30 miles northwest of Ellendale is the Whitestone Hill Historic Site, a memorial to the bloodiest battle ever fought by the U.S. Army and the Sioux in North Dakota. A distant repercussion of the Minnesota Sioux Uprising of 1862, the fighting began when Gen. Alfred Sully's expedition (mounted to punish the Indians responsible in that tragedy) encountered a Sioux buffalo-hunting party camped along the James River. A bugler stands at the apex of the hilltop monument to the 20 soldiers who died in battle. At the foot of the slope, a much smaller cairn of native stone, erected in 1942, memorializes

Wheat grows tall in the fertile soil of the beautiful Sheyenne River valley.

the 150 to 200 Sioux men, women and children killed and 156 taken captive by the force.

The State Game and Fish Department's Johnson Gulch Wildlife Management Area just south of the junction of Highways 11 and 56 preserves the "feel" of the natural wild Dakota prairie. The hilly moraines — rocky slopes sculpted of rocks and soil left behind by a melting Ice Age glacier — enclose several deep ravines. Burial mounds along the gulch have been tied to the time of Christ, while stone tepee rings can be spotted on higher ground. Bison bones are imbedded in the banks at the bottom of the gulch, a legacy of Sioux hunters who stampeded them over its rim and then slaughtered the injured animals for meat and hides.

Other Dickey County towns include **Merricourt** (17), **Fullerton** (107) and **Forbes** (84), where the legacy of early settlers ispreserved at the Tviet Shimmin Museum on Main Street.

Ashley (1,192), the McIntosh County seat, was born with the arrival of the Soo Line in 1887. Its name is drawn from Ashley Morrow, a member of the construction company which built the railway's grade. It became the seat of McIntosh County seat in 1888 after Hoskins, an older town three miles to the east on the shore of Lake Hoskins, was bypassed by the Soo; its founders gave up the fight and moved their buildings to Ashley. Today the McIntosh County Heritage Center and the privately owned Christ Rott Antique Museum display household and farming artifacts of that era. The largest local industry is Blumhardt Farm Manufacturing, a producer of implements, which was purchased by Wil-Rich of Wahpeton in 1988.

Controversy surrounds the name of **Venturia** (40). Some have said it was simply something founder John Wishek saw on the side of a derailed boxcar. It may have referred to Ventura, Cal., with its spelling eventually changed to match settlers pronunciation.

The town of **Hague** (127), named after The Hague in the Netherlands, is a reminder of the Dutch homesteaders of this area. More Dutch influence can be traced to **Hull**, named for Iowa town where the Dutch families made their first stop in America, and **Zeeland** (253), whose Dutch name means "sea land," a reference to the early prairie's resemblance to a sea of grass.

One of North Dakota's subtle pleasures is the adventure of driving down rural roads, which suddenly change from flat crop land into heavily wooded river valleys with no warning or fanfare.

Only shrubbery and a few cellars mark the site of **Winona** directly across the Missouri River from Fort Yates. In 1884 the settlement, whose name is the Sioux word for a female firstborn child, offered the variety of diversions often found near a restricted army post. When Fort Yates was abandoned in 1902, Winona felt the loss deeply and disappeared soon after.

North on U.S. 83, **Strasburg** (623) marks the division between German-Russian and Dutch settlements. Its German name was given to first to colonists' settlement in Russia, then again bestowed upon arrival in America. The sod house in which its most famous son, bandleader Lawrence Welk, was born is being restored as a centennial project.

An anecdotes tells of how **Temvik** earned its first name, Godkin: Settlers asked, "Who could possibly see much of a future in this desolate location?" An optimist answered, "God kin." It was soon renamed Brophy after its first merchant. Upon his departure in 1908, residents thought it suitable to explore new names, perhaps in honor of prominent farmers E.B. Temple or Olaf and Edward Larvik. They submitted two names, but the U.S. Postal Service refused to recognize either. Finally a compromise was hammered out at town meeting in 1911, taking half of each name to form one that has stuck ever since.

Alternate route 1804 parallels the east bank of the Missouri River, following the route of Lewis and Clark. Among sights along the way is Glencoe Church, the first Presbyterian congregation in North Dakota, organized in 1885; the now-empty building was constructed in 1885 and is now a state historic site. |||

Bismarck is a river city, and the Missouri River still has a profound effect on its residents. The Far West, a recreation of the famous river steamer, still moves through the historic waters, today carrying loads of tourists. The success of fishing has brought many to the city, where tasty walleye may be caught from the sandy bottoms.

From a few miles downstream, Bismarck seems to shimmer over the calm waters of the Missorui River. On a shady shoreline spot, a fisherman begins his day with a cup of coffee and the first cast for a walleye or northern pike.

This region is also known for its cattle industry and ethnic celebrations, such as Folkfest, Bismarck's annual September bash. Parades, dancing and eating special ethnic dinners are highlights of the week-long festival.

A few miles south of Bismarck on a high bluff overlooking the Missouri River sits the architectural masterpiece of Annunciation Priory and the nearby University of Mary. Built by a small band of Benedictine nuns in the late 1950s, the complex was designed by world renowned architect Marcel Breuer. The shadow of the 100-foot bell tower falls competely across the chapel at noon on Christmas Day, an intriguing aspect of the Priory and another example of Breuer's architectural mastery.

Beach

Medora

Dickinson

94

Mandan

22

49

New England

85

Mott

21

1806

Marmarth

Bowman

Hettinger

Fort Yates

Lariats and Longhorns

The highlights: North Dakota's West River country is a vast and lonely land of rolling hills punctuated with rough-edged buttes and meandering streams running high in May but dry in August. This is cattle country...has been since the 1880s, when Texas and Oklahoma cowboys drove herds of longhorns north to the last virgin stretch of shortgrass prairie, and since Civil War veterans established their own cattle ranches in the shelter of the Heart and Little Missouri River valleys.

The route: Beginning at Mandan, head west along Interstate 94 to Dickinson, Medora and Beach. The major southward route is U.S. 85 which, if followed past the border into South Dakota, eventually leads into the Black Hills. The return trip east may be made via U.S. 12, jogging up to N.D. 21.

Countless cities from Ohio to California claim to mark the margin of the real American West. The claim put forth by **Mandan** (15,513), though, is sounder than most. Contemporary author John Steinbeck, confronting the Missouri for the first time in 1960, sensed that the land divided here.

"Here is where the map should fold," he wrote in his classic journal *Life with Charley.* "Here is the boundary between east and west. On the Bismarck side it is eastern landscape, eastern grass, with the look and smell of eastern America. Across the Missouri on the Mandan side, it is pure west, with brown grass and water scorings and small outcrops. The two sides of the river might well be a thousand miles apart."

Not a thousand miles but nevertheless a power to be reckoned with, the Missouri marks the beginning of southwesterly North Dakota, with its working ranches and semi-arid farmlands, its legacy of the peaceful Mandan Indians and the proud fierce Sioux, its memories of George Custer and Teddy Roosevelt and cattle drives from Texas to the virgin prairie.

The ways of the cowboys among the first permanent settlers on the Missouri and the Heart are relived in Mandan on the Fourth of July during Rodeo Days. Besides its PRCA rodeo, the holiday features a parade down Main Street once led by cowboy star Gene Autry, Art in the Park, a pancake feed and street dances.

The Burlington Northern Railroad is Mandan's largest employer, everpresent since the Northern Pacific started building west in 1876. It finally bridged the Missouri in 1881; until then, trains were ferried to the western bank in summer or crossed on rails laid across the ice during the coldest months. Its red brick depot, modeled after George Washington's home Mount Vernon, is as much a landmark as Crying Hill, the east-facing slope on which locals have used white rocks to spell out the word MaNDan, with capital letters noting its central position in North Dakota.

That railroad legacy is the inspiration for the local Railroad Museum Historical Society, which is developing a museum in a depot northwest of the city exploring how those shining tracks and speeding locomotives have shaped Mandan's past and future. Retired diesel and steam locomotives sometimes take passengers for a ride around the grounds. The museum itself — with everything from dining car cutlery and china to baggage carts — is open on Sundays and summer holidays.

Mandan today has several sizeable industries. Cloverdale Foods, famed for its sausages and meats, distributes products throughout the middle west. Montana-Dakota Utilities' venerable R.M. Heskett Power Plant, which predated large-scale energy development just to the north by fully a generation, burns lignite for electricity serving land to the south and east. The Amoco Oil Refinery, too, dates back to North Dakota's first energy boom, established in 1954. The state's only operating crude oil refinery has a daily output of 58,000 barrels.

Many successful varieties of fruit trees and shelter-belt shrubs owe their gifts to the North Great Plains Research Center south of town, where guests can wander in the shade of a lush arboretum. Young people in trouble with the law live and study on the campus-like

Vain and impatient or fearless and decisive? The debate continues to this day over the merits and implications of the career of Lt. Col. George Armstrong Custer, the most well-known commander of the Seventh Cavalry at Fort Abraham Lincoln, south of Mandan. From the fort, Custer led two famous expeditions: to the Black Hills in 1874 when gold was discovered; and to the Little Bighorn in 1876.

grounds of the State Industrial School.

Modern visitors to Mandan can dine on regional specialties as different as the Seven Seas' famous South American-style steak, the Gourmet House's liver pate, and chocolate sodas and Green Rivers at the old-time soda fountain in Mandan Drug.

A 25-foot wooden Indian stands just south of the railroad tracks. Carved from a 150-year-old cottonwood log cut down nearby, it's part of sculptor Peter Toth's nationwide series of tributes to American Indians, one per state. Mandan's sculpture made North Dakota 39th in Toth's campaign.

One of North Dakota's premier attractions, Fort Abraham Lincoln State Park, lies five miles south of Mandan on N.D. 1806. Originally called Fort McKeen, this military post played a central role in the final chapters of the U.S. Army's war against the Indians, as well as the settlement of western North Dakota. It dates from 1872, when the U.S. Army stationed two infantry companies west of the Missouri to protect construction crews of the Northern Pacific Railroad. Renamed for the martyred president, Fort Abraham Lincoln was authorized in 1873 as a cavalry post. The military reservation included not only stockaded hillside blockhouses providing a panoramic view of the surrounding prairie and the Missouri and Heart River bottoms, but buildings grouped around a cavalry square on land below the bluff.

In its heyday during the middle 1870s it was occupied by 655 officers and enlisted men. At full strength, Fort Lincoln housed three companies of the Sixth and 17th Infantry, as well as six companies of the Seventh Cavalry under the command of brevet general George Armstrong Custer (who held the regular Army rank of lieutenant colonel).

From here Custer led the Seventh Cavalry to the Black Hills in 1874. Their discovery of gold on that land sacred to the Plains Indians spurred an explosion of settlement, violating the already uneasy peace of the Treaty of 1868. Hostilities continued to increase, leading to Custer's mission to Montana in 1876. He and his men rode out toward the northwest to the tune of the popular song "Garry Owen," following a trail across western Dakota marked by many monuments today. Near the Little Big Horn River in southeastern Montana they met the largest fighting force ever assembled on the Great Plains. The rest is history.

Fort Lincoln was decommissioned in 1891 and its buildings dismantled; their lumber is said to survive today in many of Mandan's older homes. Its blockhouses rose again in the 1930s, when their reconstruction was part of a Civilian Conservation Corps project that also included construction of a fieldstone museum, picnic shelters and the earth lodges of the Mandan Indians' On-a-Slant Village, which preceded the Army on this strategic site by two centuries.

Today the private Fort Abraham Lincoln Foundation has begun renovation of the fort with construction of a faithful replica of the home occupied by Custer and his accomplished wife Libby in 1874, complete with period furnishings and appointments. The group's 20-year master plan also includes reconstruction of the commissary, granary, barracks and guardhouse on Cavalry Square as well as the guardhouses of the infantry post.

A major national exhibit on the Mandans' way of life is the centerpiece of the Fort Lincoln Museum, along with information on the area's early history and occupation by white settlers. Costumed amateur actors bring the fort itself to life on summer weekends. In June it hosts a gathering of modern Seventh Cavalry units, military buffs outfitted with traditional uniforms, weapons and utensils. Several weekends in July are set aside for a walking drama, where the audience changing scenes rather than the actors: Costumed men and women act out daily life in the frontier fort. Both a Fur

Each summer, outfits from several North Dakota communities re-enact the lifestyles of the military on the western frontier. Posing on the steps of the newly completed Custer Home on Officer's Row at Fort Lincoln, the officers and enlisted men vividly recall an era of blue uniforms and hoop skirts, saddles and sabres.

Intense research by the participants insures authentic uniforms, dresses and equipment. The reconstruction of the Custer Home was a local effort that included decorating the home with authentic period furnishings. It opened for public tours during North Dakota's Centennial celebration in 1989.

At Fort Lincoln State Park, the On-A-Slant Mandan Indian village stands as a reminder of the first peoples who lived along the banks of the Missouri River. There are several reconstructed lodges on the site.

Traders Rendezvous and Homesteaders Weekend are scheduled in August; the Great American Horse Race in September.

A modern campground is nestled beneath the bluff where the Heart River joins the Missouri. Hikers set out from here along the Roughrider Trail, a designated National Recreation Trail which hugs the riverbank for the next 17 miles. Snowmobile and cross-country skiing trails are open in winter.

Travelers who head west from Mandan on Interstate 94 never pass by **New Salem** (1,081) without a second glance. The reason: New Salem Sue, the gargantuan fiberglass Holstein (32 ft. tall and 50 ft. long) that presides over the highway as a reminder of the area's dairy industry.

A historic marker nearby credits Native American wisdom as the inspiration for the local dairy industry. In 1883 homesteader John Christensen was out fighting to break the tough prairie sod just as three Indians rode over the hill. Wordless, they dismounted; the eldest bent down and turned a chunk of plowed sod so that its grass once again pointed skyward. The younger men translated his cryptic message: "Wrong side up." Though small grains survived the incident here and throughout the Missouri Slope west of the river, grazing has proven itself as good stewardship of the land. New Salem has long been the center of an important dairy region, and beef cattle outnumber humans from here far toward the west — a bit of timeless insight which sodbusters' high hopes, hard work and, often, heartache would someday reconfirm.

The Custer Trail Museum (referring to the Seventh Cavalry's route from Fort Lincoln to the Little Big Horn River) hosts visitors in a recreated village which includes a schoolhouse built in 1904, church, railroad depot, blacksmith shop and homestead shack of sandstone and scoria, as well as machinery and area antiques. It's open weekends. Sweetbriar Dam just north of New Salem was created by construction of Interstate 94. Today it has become one of best largemouth bass lakes in state, plus walleyes, bluegills and perch.

The town of **Almont** (146) lies south of I-94. It was named for the most prominent feature of the area's landscape, the Altamont Moraine, the ridge of soil and rock left as a glacier began its gradual retreat back north. The Almont HIstorical Society has established a museum on Main Street in the former office of the Almont Arena newspaper. Heritage Park features the city jail, built of native rock in 1910; a rural schoolhouse from southwest of town; the old Northern Pacific depot, and a sod house. The horse-drawn road grader used in the Almont-Sims area and the last coal car from the Sims underground mine are also on display.

One of the Missouri Slope's oldest churches, Sims Scandinavian Lutheran Church (established in 1884), still holds services nearby in the now-nearly-forgotten town of **Sims**. Originally it was a site of a siding where Northern Pacific trains stopped to take on lignite gouged from the hillside seams of Baby Mine, which supplied homes and businesses as far east as Jamestown. The town died with the removal of railroad tracks in 1947.

Glen Ullin (1,125) bears a name which combines the Gaelic word for "valley" and a favorite Scottish ballad, "Lord Ullin's Daughter." Nevertheless, the town reflects the area's predominant settlement by Germans from Russia — families recruited from Germany to settle southern Russia in the

At New Salem a landmark along Interstate 94 can be closely inspected...it's New Salem Sue, the gargantuan fiberglass Holstein that is a memorial to the area's dairy industry.

Little except a Lutheran Church remains today of Sims, a once thriving railroad town near Almont. The bricks for the original state capitol building were made here, and the town was a major stop on the Northern Pacific for water and coal. All that remains today is a peaceful valley and a church which celebrated its 100th anniversary several years ago.

1700s, only to once again take up the search for a new homeland in the latter 1800s. Saints Peter and Paul Catholic Church, built of stone and clay during the earliest settlement era, is still used for services. The Muggli Museum and Rock Shop displays petrified wood from the badlands, fossils (marine and leaf forms, including the state fossil, wood bored by prehistoric teredo worms), and handcrafted jewelry and novelties.

Lake Tschida 15 miles south is the reservoir behind Heart Butte Dam on the Heart River. Summer cabins line the shores of this manmade prairie lake, and water skiers and power boaters speed across its surface. Anglers are well represented, too. Walleyes are the most popular prey year-round, both on the lake itself and in the dam's tailrace. Hundreds of shanties appear on its ice in midwinter, with fishermen braving the cold in pursuit of walleyes and perch. Another attraction is what's reportedly North Dakota's best fishery for channel catfish.

Hebron (1078) traces its beginnings to 1884, when Germans of the St. John Evangelical Reformed Church in Chicago formed a colonization society destined for Dakota Territory. Its leader, the Rev. John Kling, asked that their chosen site's name be changed from Knife River (the Indian name, alluding to flint quarries along its banks) to Hebron, the fruitful valley in Palestine mentioned in the Bible. The town is famous for its Hebron Brick Plant, begun in 1904 with the discovery of local deposits of high-quality clay.

Just northwest of the city is the site of Fort Sauerkraut, a stockade built in 1890 to defend against Indians. It turned out to be a false alarm. Many women and children were sent to safety in Mandan on the train while men of the area — representative of the area's German-Russian roots — stored as provisions multiple barrels of sauerkraut.

Hebron is the hometown of the musical Tibors, a family of 14 siblings well-known throughout the Upper Midwest for their country and old-time music. They added their own recording studio, JoMar, onto their father's blacksmith shop in 1970.

Custer's route to Montana parallels the highway here. His wagons' tracks have been preserved by the arid climate and little human interference; you can see them near Young Man's Butte about 10 miles west of Hebron. A camp established by General Sully during the campaign that included the Battle of the Killdeer Mountains can also be found nearby.

Cathedral spires fit to grace a European capital rise above **Richardton** (699), the home of the Brothers of St. Benedict's magnificent Assumption Abbey. The saga began in 1888, when Fr. Vincent de Paul Wehrle came to Devils Lake, establishing the monastery of St. Gall. The missionary, a German immigrant himself, took a special interest in Germans from Russia whose migration to the plains of North America was then in full force. As they moved into western North Dakota, he followed them to Richardton, a center of their settlement since its establishment by the Northern Pacific in 1881.

Here Wehrle and his successors pictured a prairie Vatican of the first order, including not only a great church and monastery but a seminary to prepare young men for religious vocations. The abbey's first building was completed and blessed in 1900. It tripled as church, dormitory and college while the graceful Bavarian Romanesque cathedral dedicated to St. Mary was being built. Farmers hauled huge rocks from their fields for its for foundation; area deposits of clay and coal were baked into brick at Hebron.

When it was dedicated on Christmas Eve 1908, St. Mary's was a wonder...and easily the largest church in North Dakota. Its ornate sanctuary was brightened with jeweled light from more than 50 stained glass windows, whose cost alone was $4,500. Priests

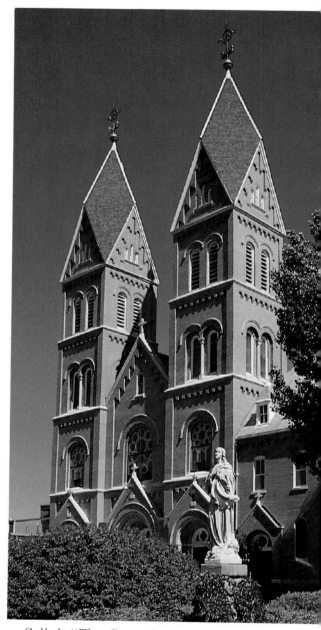

Called "The Gem of the Prairie", the Brothers of St. Benedict welcome parishioners and visitors to Assumption Abbey at Richardton.

celebrated the Latin Mass before a hand-carved altar and baldachin accented with gold leaf. Worshippers knelt beneath exquisite canvas medallions representing the 12 apostles and saints on ceiling.

Classes had begun with the new century, originally enrolling 50 students paying $14 per month. The seminary expanded with a college prep school in 1950s; by the early 1960s, 200 students were enrolled. But the school failed to thrive. The seminary was closed in 1967 and the prep school a year later. The last survivor was the junior college; it, too, ended in 1971.

Today the religious community includes about 75 men, 30 of whom live and work at the abbey, now operated as a Christian center for renewal, workshops and retreats. The community operates a 1900-acre farm, and modern print shop, and sells its private label wine for sacramental use. The abbey's museum includes a wildlife exhibit, Indian artifacts, church memorabilia, and items from pioneer days through the World Wars. The 80,000-volume college library has a strong history section including unpublished research documents.

The cemetery on its grounds contains many fine examples of iron crosses, the typical grave monuments — ornate or simple — created by blacksmiths and favored by North Dakota's German-Russian immigrants.

The land around **Taylor** (239) was among the first areas west of the Missouri to be settled by Norwegians in 1883. Just to the west, **Gladstone** (317) marks the north end of a wide band of Germans who emigrated from Hungary during the mid-1880s. Their farms extend from here south to Schefield and New England.

Dickinson (15,924) still lives up to the cowboy reputation it earned in the 1880s, when cowpokes who'd herded longhorns up from Texas came here to spend their Saturday nights. A boom town in the 1970s with the full-speed development of the petroleum

industry, it has settled back to await the coming events, when world crisis might someday revive the good times of $30-per-barrel crude. Meanwhile, the grasshopper heads of producing oil wells continue to bob on the horizon.

Local oil production reached its peak in 1984, when North Dakota wells produced 52.6 million barrels of crude. They pumped 41.3 barrels in 1987 — down, but clearly not out.

In the beginning in 1880 Dickinson was known as Pleasant Valley Siding, a tribute to its becoming site above the Heart River. The town's first merchant, H.L. Dickinson, changed its name a few years later, not in his own honor but that of his brother Wells, a senator from New York.

The booming gold fields of South Dakota helped make Dickinson's fortune as a forwarding point for freight. Thousands of German-Russian settlers poured in, thanks to the mission established here by Fr. Martin Marty. An interesting reminder of their history survives in their modern religious affiliations. From east of Dickinson area to the Missouri River, a majority are Protestant; to the west, most are Roman Catholic. The pattern reflects a similar separation maintained in the Black Sea region of Russia which they'd settled a century before. Generally people of the two Christian traditions lived in separate villages and socialized with their own kind.

These people — German by ethnic origin, but residents of southern Russia for generations before moving to America — were joined by new neighbors who shared a similar history. The area west and south of Dickinson is home to many German-Hungarians, Germans who had settled to the Danube River region of the Austro-Hungarian Empire at the invitation of Empress Maria Theresa several generations before coming to North Dakota. Dickinson's venerable German-Hungarian Club is one sign of that heritage. Other suggestions of both German traditions

Heart Butte Dam has changed the Heart River into Lake Tschida south of Glen Ullin. It is a popular vacation lake which attracts a large group of sailors virtually every summer weekend.

47

The economy and the lifestyle of western North Dakota is dependent upon cattle and petroleum. Dickinson has enjoyed a reputation as a cowtown which boomed in the early 1980s from oil development. Still, the biggest days of the week are sales days at the two livestock rings.

— German "soul food" — appear on the menus of local cafes: the cabbage soup called borscht, here traditionally thickened with cream; the thick dumpling soup called knoepfle; fleisch kuechle, fried meat-filled pastries; halupsti, cabbage rolls stuffed with ground beef and rice, and kuchen, pie-like coffee cakes of bread dough topped with cottage cheese, prunes, apricots or spiced sugar.

Dickinson lives up to its cow-town reputation each Tuesday and Thursday when area ranchers truck their livestock to Stockmen's Livestock and Western Livestock Sales. Huge numbers of cattle, hogs and sheep routinely pass through their chutes; at one, a motorcycle is used to drive livestock into and out of the sales ring.

Lignite played a large part in early settlement, heating the homes of settlers and businesses. It came from the Binek Coal Mine east of Dickinson in Lehigh (gone today), which shared its name with a more famous Pennsylvania mining town. Through the work of E.J. Babcock of the North Dakota School of Mines at UND, methods were developed to convert the low-BTU lignite to compact and efficient briquets capable of producing much higher BTUs. That legacy turns a profit today for Royal Oak, which operates a briquetting plant which turns out charcoal for backyard gourmets.

Dickinson's history is reflected in the Joachim Memorial Museum and Prairie Outpost Park on the north edge of the city, a complex of old-time structures including a pioneer-style soddy, a home built mostly of tough prairie sod. The museum also displays a sampling of dinosaur bones discovered in the Marmarth area by archeological digs directed by Dickinson State College professor Larry League.

The city's most notable native son was Doc Vincent Stickney, who in the early ranching days cured the ills of patients in an area of 50,000 square miles — from Canada to Black Hills, and Mandan to Glendive. His daughter Dorothy Stickney became a noted Broadway actress and is included in North Dakota's Rough Rider Hall of Fame.

Rocky Butte Park sets the scene for picturesque picnicking beneath a tall canopy of ponderosa pines. Patterson Lake, a reservoir on the Heart River, offers all kinds of summer recreation, including especially good spring crappie fishing. A boat launch ramp and camping facilities are available.

Belfield (1,274) was the site of Camp Houstin, a base camp during the Indian campaigns as well as a relay station on the stage route from Bismarck to Fort Keogh. The railroad arrived in 1882; in 1883 the town followed suit. Two theories surround its name: That it was inspired by the wild prairie bluebells on hills along the Heart River ("bel" being the French word for "beautiful"); or on a more mundane level, that a railroad engineer named Fields named it for his daughter Belle. The former is supported by the presence of a group of French families south of the city.

The area around north of Belfield is one of several in which Ukrainians played a leading role beginning at the turn of the century. Young people of the Veselka (Rainbow) Dancers still perform traditional folk dances at festivals today. Onion-domed Byzantine Rite and Ukrainian Orthodox churches trumpet their background; for years nuns taught catechism and the Ukrainian language in the area. St. John the Baptist Ukrainian Catholic Church in Belfield displays lovely iconastas (icons) between the sanctuary and congregation, while a second domed church nearby, St. Peter and Paul, is of the Orthodox faith. St. Demetrius Ukrainian Catholic Church is north along U.S. 85, where a hand-carved wooden cross erected in 1902 by Ukrainian settlers still stands east of the highway. Also north on U.S. 85, the Billings County Historical Society maintains the former public school in Fairfield in authentic pioneer style.

The influence of living in the Ukrainian region of Russia is still very much in evidence in Belfield. Many churches have the characteristic onion domes and displays of icons.

The popular local eatery called the Trapper's Kettle serves up homestyle cooking in a cabin-style building decorated with mounted game and ranching artifacts. Dakota Colloidal Corporation operated a plant here which processed bentonite, a badlands clay used in the manufacture of soaps.

To the north and south of Belfield along U.S. 85 is the Little Missouri National Grasslands, a 140-mile tract that's the largest of the 19 federal grasslands in the west. To the north, bighorn sheep can be spotted in Hanks Gully, at Lone Butte and along Cottonwood Creek, along with elk, antelope and deer. Tucked away in this million-acre area are the dancing ground of sharp-tailed grouse, prairie dog towns and more than a hundred eagle and falcon nests. The southern tract stretches down past Amidon to Marmarth.

Much of the land between Belfield and **South Heart** (294) was among the 10,000 acres purchased in 1910 by a syndicate of financiers in Amsterdam, Netherlands. More than 100 Dutch men and women came to work the land, complete with steam plows and European farm experts; among their crops was not only wheat by sugarbeets, potatoes, navy beans and corn. The growing seasons were hard and yields were disappointing; many returned to Europe in 1914, though some stayed on more typical family farms in the area.

A plant in the **Fryburg** oil field processes natural gas conveyed by pipeline from oil wells just outside of Theodore Roosevelt National Park.

The highway continues its unswerving westward course until suddenly the land opens up to swallow it. North Dakota's most famous peaks and valleys don't tower over the land. They lurk below it, carving the prairie from the top down. The Painted Canyon Overlook on Interstate 94 introduces the badlands, with embattled vistas of tortured buttes, broken slopes and deeply eroded valleys. Obelisks of eroded stone poke up. The badlands floor, dry as ashes, is scattered with yucca, prickly pear, odd chunks of broken stone and stumps of petrified wood, prehistoric denizens of the near-tropics turned to stone by primordial swamps and riddled with the paths of teredo worms who dined here untold millions of years ago.

Pull off to absorb the badlands' wordless challenge at the overlook. Before you is a palette of dun-and-rose sediments deposited long before the Ice Age. Rivers and streams flowing from the young Rockies laid down these layers of clay and sand and licorice-colored lignite coal. Fossil snail shells can be seen in some of the clay, along with clam, reptile and mammal skeletons and the outlines of breathtakingly ancient leaves — all 30 to 65 million years ago.

Perhaps one of the most popular views in North Dakota is Painted Canyon, a scenic overlook east of Medora on Interstate 94.

Much later, when the murky inland sea had drained away and erosion had begun, the harder and more resistant layers of sandstone became protective caps atop clay buttes, holding them firm while softer surrounding materials were swept away. The abrasive action of water and wind has gone on much longer in southwestern North Dakota than the rest of the state, which was covered by successive glaciers until about 10,000 years ago.

Chapters are still concluding here, and new ones being opened. Billings County logged the last recorded sighting of the now-extinct native Audubon bighorn sheep along Magpie Creek in 1905. Rocky Mountain bighorns were introduced into the badlands in 1956 by game management officials and — despite depradation of disease — have reestablished the herd. The long-gone elk were returned to the badlands by accident in the mid-1970s when some escaped from a herd on the Fort Berthold Indian Reservation.

Medora (94) is not only North Dakota's premier summer family resort but the site of the state's oldest tourist industry, beginning in 1879, when the Northern Pacific Railroad (which had set up camp at what was then known as Badlands Cantonment) began advertising the area to the adventurous as Pyramid Park. The railroad siding had a single hotel, the Rough Riders, whose guest list in 1883 was graced by the names of the young dude from New York, Theodore Roosevelt, and the Marquis de Mores, a French nobleman. Both arrived as hunters

50

Harold Schafer restored Medora and in so doing, helped launch the tourism industry in North Dakota. Today he remains an enthusiastic promoter of the historic cowtown.

but returned to invest time and money in the area — Roosevelt as a rancher on the Maltese Cross Ranch (and later a second, the Elkhorn), and de Mores as a rancher and entrepreneur in the meat-packing business.

The wild western cowtown never lost its dusty luster. Tom Mix, a resident for several years, was married here on horseback in 1909; both he and his bride, Olive Stokes, had just wrapped up contracts with the Miller Brothers' 101 Wild West Show. Area ranchers — some still connected with civilization only by scoria trails washed away by spring rains and closed by winter's hand — still came to town for wild old Saturday night.

But high times again loomed just ahead when Bismarck businessman Harold Schafer became the town's chief fan, promoter and benefactor. His Gold Seal Company — best known for Snowy Bleach, Glass Wax and Mr. Bubble — spearheaded the development of modern accommodations and tourist facilities as well as the Medora Musical, whose Burning Hills Singers perform in a outdoor variety show staged in a natural amphitheatre each night from June through Labor Day. A convention center and a variety of attractions — the Doll House, Wildlife and Indian Museum, and amenities from chuckwagon-style dining and ice cream parlor to several gift shops — add modern-style attractions to the historic village's appeal. Since Schafer's retirement and sale of the Gold Seal Company, its Medora operation has been directed by the non-profit Theodore Roosevelt Medora Foundation.

The State Historical Society maintains the Marquis de Mores' graceful 26-room chateau overlooking the Little Missouri River southwest of Medora, the town he founded and named for his American wife. Roman Catholic services are still held in Athenais Chapel, the small brick church in town built by Medora for her husband in 1884 and named for their daughter. A pocket-sized park downtown surrounds the heroic bronze statue of the Marquis which was erected in 1936 by Louis, Count de Villambrosa, the couple's oldest son.

The state society also looks after a ruined site and tall brick smokestack, all that remains of the Marquis' visionary beef packing plant. De Mores had planned to slaughter locally raised beef close to the prairie they fed on; he shipped his products to market in train cars cooled by blocks of ice chiseled from the meandering river. His dream of an inland cattle empire was bankrupted by consumer resistance to shipped dressed meat, their fears ignited and fanned by a coalition of railroad and eastern meat-packing interests who also cut their prices to drive him out of business. For years the packing plant's abandoned buildings stood with a sign nailed to the door: "Rent free to any responsible party who will make use of them." They were destroyed by fire in 1907.

Maintained in the manner and style of a French nobleman and his wealthy wife, the Chateau de Mores gives visitors a glimpse of a grand dream for empire.

Young Roosevelt regained his once-precarious health from the sturdy outdoors life of a badlands rancher, investing much of his future dreams beneath the big sky in the land he learned to love. His financial investment went less well. His cattle herds were wiped out in the winter of 1886-87, which marked the end of the many of the region's greatest ranches as surely as the gradual encroachment of family farmer-ranchers who eventually fenced the open range. Roosevelt went on to glory, leading his Rough Riders (including some of his badlands cronies) in the charge up San Juan Hill during the Spanish-American War and going on to become one of America's great presidents.

Roosevelt's fierce conservationist ethic led to the establishment of the National Park Service during his presidency. Ironically, though, the park that now bears his name was one of the last to receive unclouded status in that system of well-preserved wild lands.

The first effort to establish a badlands national park was mounted by area ranchers and enthusiasts in 1921, when the state Legislature passed a resolution urging the federal government to action. Years of debate extended into the Great Depression, when the government acquired large tracts of land at $2 per acre from disappointed farmers and ranchers. Civilian Conservation Corps workers laid out camping sites and trails in what became known as North Roosevelt

Arriving in Dakota Territory on September 7, 1883 for a hunting trip, Theodore Roosevelt soon purchased an interest in a cattle ranch. A desire for the vigorous life brought him back several times and caused a national park in the badlands to be named in his honor. His first ranch cabin is on display today in Medora.

Regional Park and South Roosevelt Regional Park, later administered by the U.S. Park Service as recreational demonstration areas.

Congressman William Lemke shepherded passage of a bill in 1946 which established the south unit as a national park. The north unit was added in 1948. However, they entered the system as a National Memorial Park, the only so-named area in the country. That undefined status (always nebulous, but viewed as an obstacle to increased tourism) was upgraded in 1978 to full rank as Theodore Roosevelt National Park.

It now includes not only the two original units separated by 45 miles of U.S. Highway 85, but the remote site of Roosevelt's Elkhorn Ranch at a midpoint along the Little Missouri River. The cabin from his Maltese Cross stands near the South Unit entrance and interpretive center in Medora.

Explore the breathtaking landscape of the south unit along winding auto routes as well as hiking trails (including the popular favorite overlooking Wind Canyon) and horse paths. Guided or unguided horseback expeditions begin at Peaceful Valley Ranch inside the park, where saddle horses may be rented. Like Medora, the ranch comes by its tourism credentials honestly; the nation's first dude ranch, the Custer Trail, was established here by the Eaton Brothers in the 1880s. Cottonwood Campground nearby provides fully modern and primitive campsites for RV and tent camping.

Herds of bison, elk, bighorn sheep, whitetail and mule deer, pronghorn antelope and wild horses roam the park today, though the original Audubon bighorn sheep and grizzly bears are no longer seen here. Audacious prairie dogs stand sentry over extensive tracts of burrows, preening in the sun and growing fat on tidbits supplied (against Park Service orders) by charmed tourists. This is the prairie dog version of the Good Life: Elsewhere in ranching country they're shot or poisoned as pests.

Sully's Creek State Recreation Area two miles south of Medora offers primitive campsites in the shelter of a twisted cliff of sandstone south of Medora. Interconnecting trails allow hikers and riders on horseback to explore the nearby Little Missouri National Grasslands as well as Roosevelt Park. West of Medora, Buffalo Gap Campground offers fully modern campsites.

The flat-topped mountain from which **Sentinel Butte** (86) takes its name testifies to several elements of the area's heritage. Fossil fish once found in the rock at its summit (now scarce due to a century of collectors) suggest the prehistoric swamps that once overlaid the badlands area. Its name is said to have come from two Arikara Indian scouts with Custer's forces killed here in a skirmish with the Sioux en route to the Little Big Horn, though other stories -- romantic and otherwise -- have also had their day. Today

microwave and radio towers dominate the summit, linking the remote ranch country to the entire world.

Sentinel Butte is the home of Fiddlin' Bill Johnson and cowboy poet and illustrator Bill Lowman, whose publications include "*Riders of the Leafy Spurge*" and "*The Blueberry Roan*." Johnson, who spearheaded the Old-Time Fiddlers Jamboree held annually at the International Peace Garden, is considered the dean of North Dakota fiddlers.

The Home on the Range for Boys northwest of Sentinel Butte is a 1,070-acre working ranch for wayward boys. It was established by Father Elwood Cassedy in 1950 with support from North and South Dakota Eagles Clubs. The ranch hosts the annual Champions' Ride Rodeo the first Sunday in August. Set in a natural amphitheatre among the buttes, it's one of the largest one-day rodeos in the country.

With the rugged and mostly inaccessable hills offering shelter, wildlife have once again flourished in the badlands. Shy Bighorn sheep blend with the clay buttes so well they are often overlooked by passing motorists.

Since Texas herds were first trailed into the area, the badlands has been cattle country. Today's breed of cowboy is still very much like the original...tough people working in hard country.

Beach (1,381), the Golden Valley County seat, was named for Capt. Warren Beach, a member of the 11th Infantry which escorted surveyors for the Northern Pacific Railroad in 1873. The area sits on the Fort Union formation, with its petroleum and lignite resources; much uranium exploration took place here 30 years ago. Beef and dairy cattle graze the surrounding prairie; the latter provide raw material for Valley Dairy Products, a local cheese plant.

Beach is the site of the Golden Valley County Historical Museum. It occupies a renovated garage across from the courthouse, with extensive displays depicting the county's history from dinosaur days through Indian days and the pioneer era. An authentically restored 1909 one-room school is also on the grounds.

The enormity of emptiness here on the western edge of Dakota is suggested by the near-complete absence of settlements on the road map between Beach and Alexander, some 70 miles north. Only **Trotters** (north of Beach on N.D. 16) remains of the dozen-odd settlements that sprang up in the early 20th century but have since disappeared; its post office, too, is scheduled to close upon the retirement of postmaster Leonard Hall, whose rural mail route serves only a few ranch families, yet covers an area with a radius of 50 miles. To the south of Beach, **Golva** (101) -- founded in 1915 -- also survives. Its name combines the first letters of GOLden VAlley County.

Head south of Interstate 94 on U.S. Highway 85 at Belfield, and you'll travel stark but mighty country straight to the Black Hills. People are sparse here, but those you meet are universally friendly and helpful in that famous spirit of the West.

If you think a town called **New England** (895), 12 miles east of U.S. 85 along N.D. 21, sounds out of place on the high dry prairie, consider how much more so its original moniker might have been: Mayflower. It was established as a colony of Yankees who arrived in a group of 50 families in 1887; in later years Germans from Russia and other groups came to predominate the area. Slope County's oldest town was laid out with furrows plowed in prairie sod. At one time New England shipped more wheat than any other point on the railroad line, with five bustling grain elevators. They've since been closed or absorbed into one regional farmers' cooperative.

Named for U.S. District Judge Charles Amidon of Fargo, **Amidon** (43) is the seat of Slope County government, distinguished as one of the most sparsely populated spots in the United States, and thinly settled even in a state that ranks 46th in population. (Only Billings and Sioux have slightly fewer residents.)

The Burning Coal Vein, now smoldering deep in the earth, already smoldered when the first white men arrived in the area. Ignited by lightning or a prairie fire, it eats at a deep seam of lignite 30 feet underground. Its fumes are believed to have influenced the growth of the unique columnar junipers growing above ground. These unseen fires have since prehistoric times baked the native clay into a red brick called porcellanite, locally known as scoria -- a fine and practical material much used on badlands roads.

Near the burning vein, the historic Logging Camp Ranch offers visitors a unique vacation experience along the scenic Little Missouri River. Once the site of pioneer rancher A.C. Huidekoper's horse operation, the Hanson family now opens the working ranch to guests. They're housed in rustic log cabins built of the ranch's ponderosa pines. Campsites accommodate both tents and RVs. Proprietor John Hanson also owns Dakota Waters Resort on Beulah Bay.

Every now and then, as they do throughout North Dakota, an antique threshing machine appears on the horizon, standing at the top of a rolling hill. These mechanical dinosaurs,

Near Amidon and Marmath, the remains of dinosauers may be found. From the fanciful mechanical threshers that decorate hilltops, to serious amateur paleontologists who search for dinosauers bones, like Mike Lutens of Marmath (top left). The lower reaches of the badlands offers fancinating contrasts. West of Amidon at the historic Logging Camp Ranch, rustic cabins are the vacation destination for hunters and people seeking the solitude of a pine forest in the badlands.

their placement and meanings are personal statements by landowners who recall the pre-combine era of steam threshing rigs as a landmark in time.

White Butte ten miles south of Amidon is the highest point in North Dakota, standing 3,506 feet above sea level. If the state were a broad, flat platter, this southwest corner would be the higher rim, with the Red River puddling out from its lowest point at Pembina in the northeast, fully half a mile below.

Bowman (2,071), briefly called Eden, was founded in 1907 with the arrival of the Chicago, Milwaukee and Puget Sound Railroad. Both the city and the county is serves owe their name to prominent territorial legislator William Bowman. Perhaps the first of western North Dakota's bonanza cattle ranches was established near here in 1878.

Two campsites near Bowman, Butte View State Campground and Twin Buttes Campground, both offer tent and RV camping sites.

Your chance for record walleyes is good at Bowman-Haley Reservoir south of town on the Grand River. A 14-pounder was taken several years ago; Game and Fish Department experts contend that most of the lake's lunkers actually die of old age! Northerns of up to 20 pounds have been reported.

Several points of interest lie west of Bowman on U.S. 12 including Fort Dilts Historic Site, an expanse of prairie broken only by five marked graves. Fort Dilts was not a military post, but a hastily-built ramparts of prairie sod thrown up by a wagon train attacked by hostile Sioux in 1864. The 80-wagon caravan, headed by Capt. James Fisk, was bound for the gold fields of Montana. Inside the soddy breastworks, they managed to hold off the Indians for two weeks until help arrived from Fort Rice. The site was named after Corp. Jefferson Dilts, a scout who died in the skirmishes; 13 of the party of 50 lost their lives here.

Rhame (222), the highest town in North Dakota (elevation-wise), is cradled between two tall scoria-topped buttes. It's the site of one of the state's 12 natural gas processing plants. The area lies in the Little Beaver Dome, one of the nation's richest natural gas fields; its gas has been conveyed by pipeline to cities in western North Dakota for most of the current century.

The pride and joy of **Marmarth** (190) is its fully restored turn-of-the-century Mystic Theatre believed to be the oldest in the state, where the local amateur theatre group performs each fall. It was built in 1914 expressly for motion pictures. The St. Charles Hotel is also being restored as a museum by the Marmarth Historical Society.

The Marmarth area's first bona fide tourist was Theodore Roosevelt, who shot both his first grizzly and his first buffalo near here along Little Beaver Creek in 1884. The town itself dates back to 1902. Its name is an amalgamation of Margaret Martha Fitch, granddaughter of the president of the Chicago, Milwaukee and St. Paul Railroad, which built a roundhouse here on its way to Seattle. One of Marmarth's modern landmarks is the Past Time Bar, whose owner Mike Lutens has participated on some of the many dinosaur digs sponsored by the Universities of Michigan and North Dakota, the Milwaukee Public Museum, Dickinson State College and others.

Archaeologists and paleontologists make tracks each summer to the dinosaur fields among the cacti, rattlesnakes and exposed rock of the Hell Creek formation near Marmarth. Once this was a 400-mile-wide inland sea extending into southeastern Montana and northwestern South Dakota, its shores ringed with towering redwoods, moss-draped cypress, lush underbrush...all 65 million years ago.

With or without permits from the federal government (which manages much of these grasslands) or the state of North Dakota,

Two famous landmarks in Marmath are the Mystic Theatre (above) where theatrical productions are still performed, and the ever increasing search for dinosauer remains. Scientists gently uncover a triceratops bone north of the old railroad town.

by Sue Blunt, Dickinson

researchers have been harvesting the half-exposed bones of giants that once roamed the earth. Perhaps their most outstanding find was the 1987 discovery of a rare full skeleton of Triceratops, a horned dinosaur weighing six tons and measuring 30 feet from beak to tip of tail. Leg bones, claws and teeth of Tyrannosaurus Rex have also been located here. Other finds include bones of Anatosaurus, a flat-headed, duck-billed dinosaur from the family Hadrosaurus; Dromaeosaurus, which resembled the modern flightless birds like the ostrich; Struthiomimus, 12 feet long and even more bird-like; Herperornis, a four-foot diving bird on the order of the loon; Leidyosuchus, a speedy crocodile with a six-foot head that dined on birds, and miscellaneous giant turtles, reptiles and prehistoric monsters.

Most of the bones excavated from the area have been pirated away to museums and research facilities around the country. The '87

Triceratops, for example, can be seen at the Cranbrook Institute in Detroit. Dickinson State College archaeologists are leading a drive for museums to house their growing collections both in Marmarth and on their campus.

Other Bowman County town titles offer a sample of intriguing roots. East on N.D. Highway 12 are **Scranton** (415), named for Scranton, Pa., where coal is also mined, and **Gascoyne** (23), originally called Fischbein, perhaps after one of the 75 Jewish families who attempted to homestead here in 1910; the area today is home to many Bohemians (descended from early coal miners) and Poles. The vanished village of **Paoli** was named for Pasquale de Paoli, the Corsican patriot. **Stillwater** bears the name of the picturesque river town in Minnesota; **Utopia** was named not for heaven, but for Texas.

Knife River Coal's Gascoyne Mine supplies lignite to Otter Tail Power's Big Stone Station

at Milbank, S.D. American Colloid operates a briquetting plant at Gascoyne, turning out charcoal briquets from lignite mined nearby by North American Coal. Scranton was once the site of a thriving brick plant, whose products can still be seen in many local buildings. Longhorns driven north to badlands pasture along the Texas Chisholm Trail passed directly by the site of the (much later) Milwaukee Road depot.

Lookout Point in Adams County two miles from **Reeder** (355) offers a view of five townsites — Reeder, Bucyrus, Gascoyne, Scranton and Buffalo Springs. In the distance at the Whetstone Buttes, a high ridge of hills topped by sandstone so hard that pieces were used by Indians and early settlers for sharpening their tools and weapons.

Bucyrus (32) was named after the steam shovel used to build the Chicago St. Paul and Milwaukee Railroad grade in 1908.

Regent sits amid the splendor of cropland and the wide open spaces usually associated with western North Dakota.

Hettinger (1,739) is the county seat of Adams County. Mott of course serves the same function in Hettinger County, but all is not as confusing as it seems; Adams was created out of Hettinger in 1907, leaving the name behind. Both were christened by territorial legislator E.A. Williams for his father-in-law, Mathias Hettinger of Illinois.

Hettinger's Dakota Buttes Historical Society Museum, open by appointment, features more than 15,000 photographs from southwestern North Dakota history and artifacts from the area's pioneer days. Dakota Packing here processes North Dakota beef, while a State Experiment Station conducts research in sheep grazing and crops. Hettinger was the home of Ole Abelseth, North Dakota's only survivor of the *Titanic*.

The Cedar River National Grasslands southeast of Hettinger along the North and South Dakota border offers naturalists an untouched laboratory for spotting prairie grasses, flowers and wildlife, including antelope and mule deer. Nature coexists with mining of lignite at Sheep Creek near Haynes; it's used as home heating fuel.

The last great buffalo hunt in the United States took place near **Haynes** (58) in 1882. Some 600 Indians from Standing Rock under the direction of Indian Agent James McLaughlin took part in the killing of ten percent of a herd estimated at 50,000 bison. Only a few months later, in 1883, hunters and wildlife experts began to realize that the once-numberless American bison was virtually extinct. Today's total in all North America — living without exception in parks and wildlife preserves — does not exceed the number of animals galloping with that single great herd near Haynes.

Regent (297) is north of Haynes along N.D. 8. The Hettinger County Historical Society Museum on Main Street includes the Dr. W. W. Hill Drugstore (named to the National Register of Historic Places), a former cafe divided into period rooms depicting a turn-of-

the-century household, Zion Evangelical Lutheran Church (moved here from Burt) and Frontierland, a re-created pioneer street housed in an enormous steel building. It's open Wednesday afternoons. Regent is the home town of U.S. Congressman Byron Dorgan.

While coal is associated more frequently with the so-called "energy country" along the south shore of Lake Sakakawea, Hettinger County too has its lignite outcroppings. **Mott** (1,315), the Hettinger County seat, is named for the immigration agent for the Northern Pacific, which led to its settlement in 1904. For some obscure but fascinating reason — perhaps a forgotten native son who went to work for Rand McNally — Mott appears on many globes that bypass more luminous cities like Minneapolis. Postmaster Robert

Kammen has written many western novels for Zebra Books.

East on N.D. 21 past **Burt** and **Bentley**, travelers enter Grant County. The "old Leipzig" suggested by the name of **New Leipzig** (352) is not Leipzig, Germany, homeland of some of the German-Russians who settled the area, but an earlier settlement near Antelope Butte bypassed by the Northern Pacific in 1910. Residents of that older town (simply called Leipzig) moved their establishments to the new city 11 miles away. Hope Lutheran Church, built by German-Russian settlers in 1897, is still standing near the older site.

Elgin (930) was called Shanley (after John Shanley, bishop of the diocese of Fargo) until the arrival of the Milwaukee Road in 1910. The railroad objected to its similarity to

Once intended as a waterhole for thirsty steam locomotives, today Mirror Lake in Hettinger is a popular swimming and picnic area only a few blocks from downtown.

Stanley. During the interminable debate that followed, one resident is said to have glanced at his wristwatch and said, "Let's name it Elgin!" The Grant County Historical Society operates a museum in the former Northern Pacific depot which features area Indian artifacts and homestead-era antiques; a Lutheran church which originally stood near Heil has been moved to the grounds and fully restored. The society has also restored a fieldstone church north of town to its original glory.

For many years, the hieroglyphic-carved Medicine Rock, eight miles southeast of Elgin — now a historic site — was the scene of Indian pow wows and ceremonies to invoke the support of the Great Spirit in hunting the buffalo. Food and trinkets were left in a cleft of the rock as sacrifices to the gods. The dance circle west of the site is still worn into the dry prairie, testimony to thousands of dancers' feet across untold years.

A sod church called Wasse Kirche was long a center of community activity for the German-Russian families who settled around **Heil**.

Just past **Leith** (59) is the Grant County seat of **Carson** (469). It draws its name from not one but three pioneer businessmen, Frank Carter and the Pederson brothers...and from not one but three townsites. Old Carson stood roughly on the south edge of the present city; North Carson was two miles north. When the railroad came through in 1910 it passed almost exactly between the two — both of which were moved to the final location. Carson's downtown today has been spruced up in step with a wild west theme, complete with a sheltered boardwalk, thanks to the generosity of a native boy who moved away and made his fortune in computers.

A historic plaque marks the site of the Carson Roller Mill, established in 1913 by miller Clarence Mott and operated for 50 years by Vincent Muggli. It's a reminder of North Dakota's long quest for industrial development. At the turn of the century experienced millers often escaped the rat race of Minneapolis' giant flour industry by looking for backers in small towns across Dakota. They generally had little trouble raising the capital to build a small mill to serve the local market.

The Grant County Historical Society operates a museum in Carls School northeast of Carson; it was the county's last one-room school to close its doors.

The Cannonball Stage Station southeast of Carson marked the Northwestern Express stage line's crossing point of the Cannon Ball River en route from Bismarck to the Black Hills. The route carried goldseekers from the Northern Pacific railhead to Deadwood, S.D., where gold was discovered in 1874. One-way fare was $23. Wheel ruts still mark the path, both here and at a second historic site on the east edge of Flasher, where Concord stages carried thousands of passengers during the

The landscape of southwestern North Dakota is dominated by lush and hearty natural grasslands, making it one of the nation's prime producers of livestock.

years from 1877 to 1880.

Other Grant County towns include **Lark** (honoring not the North Dakota state bird but a settler named Larkee), **Raleigh** (once known as Dog Tooth for the jagged sandstone buttes nearby), **Freda** and **Shields**. The Grant County Historical Society has developed a local museum in the 1917 St. Gabriel Catholic Church there. A new addition to the grounds is the log cabin built by Maj. James McLaughlin, Indian agent at Fort Yates, on his daughter Imelda's homestead allotment. The logs, held together by wooden pegs and square nails, has been

moved from the Circle M Ranch to a site next to the church.

Flasher (410) was headquarters for the Brown Land Company, which established the townsite in 1902 along with many others in southwestern North Dakota. He named it for his niece and secretary Mabel Flasher. Along with the predominately German-Russian settlers who settled the area in the early 1900s was a colony of a dozen Jewish families who homesteaded near here in the early 1900s, but whose enterprises ended in failure.

The privately owned Meyer Hunting Preserve near Flasher offers pheasant hunting from September through March. Two other operations in the vicinity also manage private herds — Johnson Elk Ranch and Rossow Buffalo Ranch. The original Northwest Express stage station now serves as the city library and museum.

St. Anthony was once known as Littleheart, thanks to Little Heart Butte north of the city. When a group of Catholic German-Russians settled the area in 1887, they eventually named it after their church. Like so many towns in North Dakota's German-Russian triangle, St. Anthony remains predominantly Catholic; others have stayed mostly protestant. The segregation can be traced back to the colonizing groups who settled the area, often led by priests or clergymen; towns of the Catholic and Protestant faiths literally alternated along the line as the railroads opened up new lands.

South on N.D. Highway 6, the name of **Breien** offers a hint of Norwegian antecedents. A pioneer settler named Jacobson christened the town after his family name back in the oldcountry.

The Cannonball River marks the northwest boundary of Sioux County. Despite its name and the fact that it is part of the Standing Rock Reservation, most farms in Sioux County are operated by white families dating back to 1913, the year the reservation was opened to settlement.

The site where gold seekers were ambushed by Indians is peaceful today, unlike the terror experienced there in 1864. (Below) Elk are flourishing in the hidden draws of the badlands.

Solen (138) is named for the first school teacher working among the Sioux of the Standing Rock Reservation, daughter of Honore Picotte, a French fur trader of aristocratic lineage who came up the Missouri in 1825, and Eagle Woman All Look At, a Sioux woman. Former Solen schoolteacher Kathleen Eagle has established a growing reputation as a popular author of romance novels.

Selfridge was incorporated in 1919. It may have been named for Thomas Selfridge, a World War I Army aviator, for a Soo Line official or after the ridge of hills which surrounds the town.

In 1977 persistent reports of a Bigfoot-like creature drew interest to the Solen, Fort Yates and Little Eagle areas. Tracks 16-18" long and six feet apart — foot with five toes and spur-like formation on outside joint. No conclusions were drawn.

A monument overlooking Lake Oahe tells the legend of Standing Rock, a chunk of

The memorial to the Standing Rock is central to the legends of the Sioux which live at Fort Yates. (Below) A memorial to medicine man Sitting Bull, who lived on the Grand River after his surrender effectly ended the Indian Wars in 1881.

granite that gives the reservation its name. The famous Sioux landmark was said to resemble a Sioux woman and her child who refused to accompany their tribe on a journey; when the rest returned to find them, only the boulder remained.

The Standing Rock Indian Agency was established in 1875, when a U.S. Army garrison was stationed here; the military post known as Fort Yates was not established until 1889, when it replaced Fort Rice 40 miles further north. Its name and that of the town of **Fort Yates** (771) reflect that of Capt. George Yates, killed with Custer in the Battle of the Little Big Horn. Ironically, here Sitting Bull — among the victors in that battle — spent his last years. The fort was abandoned in 1903. Standing Rock was opened for general settlement in 1913.

A monument to Sitting Bull stands at the entrance to Fort Yates, acknowledging the great leader of the Teton Sioux. After Indian forces defeated the Seventh Cavalry, he and hundreds of his followers eventually fled to Canada; they returned, dispirited and hungry, to surrender at Fort Buford in 1881. At Standing Rock, the great Indian leader was active in the messianic movement called the Ghost Dance, prohibited and feared by the Indian agents. That support led to his killing during an attempted arrest by Indian police in 1890. The marker stands over one of several burial places of his remains, which have been stolen and reclaimed repeatedly in the past hundred years. Another local monument honors the police who died in the incident.

Fort Yates was also the home of the late blacksmith Louis Snider, the last of the area's great German-Russian artisans famous for their ornate iron cross-shaped grave markers.

Heading north on N.D. 24, travelers once again cross the Cannon Ball River, after which the town of **Cannon Ball** was named. It owes its name from the perfectly rounded spheres of limestone swept along its course.

The **Huff** area played a central role in the Mandan Indian religion — roughly that of the Garden of Eden. Legend told that the first people lived underground until, led by the chief Good Furred Robe, they climbed a vine to the surface. Tradition suggested that the ancient village at Huff, whose lodge rings can be made out today, was their first home.

A state historic site eight miles southeast of Huff marks the location of Fort Rice, the Army post built by General Alfred Sully during his campaign against the Sioux in 1864 and occupied until 1884. Sully's force traveled the Missouri River to this point, then moved west to fight the Battles of Killdeer Mountain and the Badlands. The fort defended not only the area's first settlers but wagon trains heading overland for the Montana gold fields. From here Col. Dill and 600 men rode west to rescue the Fisk expedition under siege at the hasty battlements of Fort Dilts near present-day Rhame.

In 1868 Fort Rice hosted a peace conference that led to signing of the Laramie Treaty. The stage was set when Sitting Bull agreed to meet with the one white man he trusted, Fr. Pierre Jean De Smet, the Jesuit missionary he knew as Black Robe. Sitting Bull's position was clear: "Move out the soldiers and stop the steamboats, and then we shall have peace." Nevertheless, at the priest's urging Sitting Bull sent two representatives, Chief Gall and Bull Owl, to the peace talks.

The treaty that ensued guaranteed large sections of the west, including the sacred Black Hills, would remain the Indians' domain. Its violation — inspired in large part by Custer's 1874 discovery of gold in those mountains — led to both the Battle of the Little Big Horn and the acrimonious stand-off the Black Hills today between the government and Indians who insist that they still own the region. III

61

To Crosby

Williston

(1804)

Fort Union

Fort Buford

Lift Bridge

(58)

(200)

(85)

(1806)

(23)

Garrison

THEODORE ROOSEVELT
NATIONAL PARK
NORTH UNIT

Lost Bridge

Lake

Sakakawea

(22)

Knife River

Fort Mandan

Little Missouri River

Killdeer

(200)

Beulah

Hazen

Cross Ranch

THEODORE ROOSEVELT
NATIONAL PARK
SOUTH UNIT

(85)

(48)

(25)

(1806)

(94)

Dickinson

Richardton

Mandan

Fort Lincoln

Gateway To The Great Northwest

The highlights: Much of North Dakota's part in our nation's history was played out in the northwest corner of the state. Here representatives of the great American fur companies struck bargains with mountain men, Indians and soldiers at the confluence of the Missouri — the Indians' great "Smoky Water" — and the Yellowstone River. Here farmers plotted to break the grain market's headlock on their fortunes through the leftist Nonpartisan League, decried in national editorials as the "red glow on the northern horizon." And here in more recent times have engineers and oil-field roughnecks mingled with wheat farmers and ranchers...all dependent on the riches underfoot in the Williston Basin.

The route: Beginning at Williston, explore the confluence of the Missouri and Yellowstone Rivers. Then trace a loop through the part of the state with the most pervasive Norwegian accent eastward to Tioga, north to Crosby and down again via U.S. 85. South of Williston, U.S. 85 carries you past Watford City to the Killdeer Mountains and the north unit of Theodore Roosevelt National Park. Angle east on N.D. 200 through North Dakota's energy heartland. Then follow the shoreline of Lake Sakakawea around the point toward the north and west, returning to Williston along the shoreline of the big lake.

Welcome to **Williston**, a strategic point in the history of what railroad baron James J. Hill came to call the Great Northwest. In length, its tales of white settlement rival those of Pembina in northeastern North Dakota, with both corners probed by explorers and trod by fur traders at the opening curtain of the nineteenth century.

In national significance the Williston area goes even farther. The confluence of the Yellowstone and Missouri Rivers lent geographical impact. The colliding interests of international politics breathed urgency into the exploration of the Upper Missouri and the land that lay between here and the Pacific Ocean. The mercantile giants of America clashed here to harvest furs and robes of the mountains and plains from their native customers hungry for "civilization's" wares — Assiniboin and Blackfeet, Sioux and Arikara, Mandan, Hidatsa and Crow.

Lewis and Clark pushed up the Missouri River in 1804 and cruised back down toward St. Louis in 1806. Their mission: observing the land and testing the waters for President Thomas Jefferson, who'd acquired it from Napoleon in 1803 as part of the greatest land deal in recorded history. Others rode in their wake, carried north by steamboats like the *Yellow Stone* (which docked at Fort Union in 1832) — American artists John James Audubon and George Catlin and the Swiss painter Karl Bodmer, as well as titled Europeans including Prince Maximilian of Wied and Prince Paul Wilhelm of Wurttemberg.

Lewis and Clark's journey can be traced today along North Dakota Highways 1804 and 1806, where highway markers highlight experiences from their voyage of discovery. Capt. Clark stood at the junction of the two great rivers in 1806 and observed that it was a "judicious position for the purpose of trade." A total of nine forts would share that judgment as the 1800s proceeded. Two grew to enormous prominence — Fort Union, the trading post of the American Fur Company, and the U.S. Army's Fort Buford, a key outpost in the last years of the war between the Army and the Indians.

The city of Williston (13,336) is much younger than the legends that surround it. Its modern legacy can be traced to the Great Northern Railroad (then still called the St. Paul, Minneapolis and Manitoba Railway) which arrived from Minot in 1887 during one of the fastest track-laying frenzies of all time. Hill called the settlement "Williston" in honor of friend and stockholder S. Willis James of New York City, who'd accompanied him on a rather dreary trip west that same year. (The James family sent the city a gracious thank-you gift — the town library.)

Its beginnings, though, go further back to the days of Fort Buford, when it sprang up as Little Muddy, a rough wide-open encampment of the sort that flourished just outside most western military reservations. Its first families were those of men who cut hay for the fort's horses and wood to fire the boilers of steamboats plying the Missouri and Yellowstone. Mail carrier and frontier scout Yellowstone Kelly built the first log hut on the ground where Williston would one day stand.

With statehood Williston became the county seat of Williams County which, along with Divide County, makes up one of most thoroughly Norwegian parts of state. That background dates to the first decade of the twentieth century, the last days of free land under the Homestead Act: Here in northwestern North Dakota and northeastern Montana was the last chance to carve out a farm solely through sweat rather than money. Many of the area's Scandinavian-born farmers came not directly from the Old Country but from Minnesota and Wisconsin, as well as the Red River Valley.

Hill dreamed of turning the northwest into a Garden of Eden similar to the farm towns of the old Midwest — a vision that not only would offer a bountiful home to hopeful settlers, but would also guarantee profits to his railroad. Hill had to be hard-nosed. Unlike the builders of the Northern Pacific, he had no colossal federal gift of free land with which to finance his line; he was forced by prudence as well as pride to keep a sharp eye on the bottom line. There were chinks in his sturdy logic, though, none more troublesome than the climate. This arid Eden's fertile soil was dampened by no more than 13 inches of rainfall each year, making each year's harvest notoriously dependent on the weather. The nearby town of **Bonetraill** — established in 1905 — reflects local settlers' first cash "crop," the buffalo bones that littered the landscape, preserved by the bone-dry prairie.

The Missouri River, now a mile from the city's center, once flowed past the end of Main Street. Out beyond the limits, the flat fertile landscape is punctuated with oil drilling rigs and bobbing wells as well as Minuteman missile sites poking up from the prairie amidst necklaces of barbed wire.

Williston has experienced cycles of boom times and bad since the discovery of oil in the Williston Basin in the '50s. Those tides have surged with the gravitational pull of volatile Arabian sheiks and multinational petroleum princes. Less glamorous and somewhat more stable is the market for lignite, the crumbly dark-brown coal one step up from peat that lines much of the basin; deposits stretch from here east to Velva and south to Scranton and Haynes. The Geo Resources Mine southeast of the city produces not coal, however, but a drilling mud additive used in oil exploration. Two of North Dakota's 12 natural gas processing plants are in the Williston area, with another near Trenton. In 1959 the Hardy Salt Company began mining another of the basin's resources, salt; it was subsequently sold to Diamond Crystal and then International Salt, which closed the operation in 1988.

Progressive and civic-minded, the Williston area was the site of New School District #1, first major reorganized and consolidated district in the state. The national Farmers Union named this the Cooperative City of North Dakota in the 1930s, when it boasted not only a cooperative creamery but an oil

An exact replica of Fort Union's bourgeois house is an interpretive center documenting the fur trade - the first wave of free enterprise on the western frontier that was headquartered at the confluence of the Yellowstone and Missouri rivers.

plant, a primary grain warehouse and a poultry plant operated under the same system of member ownership. The campus of the University of North Dakota-Williston offers area students a two-year program of junior college and vocational classes.

Among the biggest events of the civic year are the Prairie Arts Festival in June, NDRA Rodeo in July, and Upper Missouri Valley Fair in August. Williston is the home of Virgil Hill, World Boxing Association light heavyweight champion and winner of a silver medal during the 1984 Summer Olympics.

The Williams County Frontier Museum is located at Spring Lake Park three miles north of the city; it's open on summer Sundays and special occasions. On its grounds are a rural church dating from 1919 and two blockhouses, along with a 1908 home, an 1887 grocery store, a fully equipped old-time dental office, a country school and an old wooden windmill. The park also encompasses two fishing lakes, picnic facilities and a playground.

Hungry Gulch 25 miles east of Williston was the site of the brief Dakota Gold Rush in 1910. The excitement died as quickly as it was set ablaze by settler James Moorman's discovery of gold-colored rocks on his property. They turned out to be iron pyrite, or "fool's gold." Nevertheless, Moorman did profit handsomely from the appetite for gold by selling ravenous gold-diggers countless plates of flapjacks made of flour from his well-stocked larder.

Lewis and Clark State Park 19 miles southeast of Williston sprawls along the Lake Sakakawea shoreline amid towering buttes and sloping hills. Its modern boating facilities include a marina, boat ramp and concessions. A self-guided nature trail permits campers to glimpse white-tailed and mule deer, pheasants, porcupines, sharp-tail grouse and chipmunks. In winter, park trails accommodate snowmobiles and cross-country skiers.

The Snowden Bridge still spans the Missouri River west of Williston and until recently was used for both rail and vehicle traffic. It was built as a lift-span bridge to allow for river navigation.

The waters near the park and the upper bays of Lake Sakakawea have become world famous among freshwater fishermen. More walleyes over eight pounds are taken near Williston than in all the rest of the state combined, as well as good catches of saugers and northern pike. During the spring paddlefish season on the river above Williston, anglers have snagged specimens of more than 100 pounds.

Fort Union National Historic Site is 25 miles southwest of Williston just past **Trenton**, named by Great Northern stockholders for the city in New Jersey. The National Park Service's accelerated program of reconstruction and interpretation has turned Fort Union into a first-class destination for those interested in the fur trade. Here — 1,900 miles upriver from St. Louis as the river travels — was one of the most strategic sites of the American fur trade era. First occupied by fur traders William Ashley and Andrew Henry in 1822, the spot was chosen once again in 1828 by Kenneth McKenzie of American Fur Company's Upper Missouri Outfit. He'd reign over this most important and well-defined trading post for the next 30 years, living as a high-born gentleman in the midst of the wilderness and earning the nickname "King of the Upper Missouri."

Today the park service has reconstructed the palatial (by prairie standards) home of the bourgeois, or chief trader, as a visitors center just inside the rebuilt palisades. Additional buildings and stone bastions are scheduled for coming years. The entire archeological and restoration project has been funded by a $1.7 million appropriation by the federal government; additional funds are being raised privately by a group headed by Lord John Jacob Astor VIII, a direct descendant of American Fur Company founder.

Ongoing archeological research offers visitors a chance to watch professionals painstakingly recapture bits of the past. Thousands attend the annual Mountain Men Rendezvous each Fourth of July weekend.

Just east of Fort Union is Fort Buford, the military post established in 1866 as part of chain of fortifications extending from Fort Leavenworth to the Columbia River. Its first company faced continual skirmishes with Indians during that first winter. Rumors were widely circulated that the entire company had been massacred and that its commander, Capt. William Rankin, had killed his own wife to keep her from falling into the hands of the enemy. The next summer a new five-company post of adobe was built in the shadow of a burly 12-foot stockade (which used materials salvaged from Fort Union, by then abandoned).

Fort Buford was under constant siege in its early days. Raids on woodcutting, haying and hunting parties were so frequent that men seldom left without armed guards. Soldiers were instructed to police the region to prevent traders from selling illegal whiskey and ammunition to hostile Indians, and to distribute annuities to friendly tribes in area.

After Custer's defeat at the Little Big Horn in 1876, the fort became an important supply depot for entire region. The Sioux leader Sitting Bull surrendered here in 1881 and was

The annual Buckskinner Rendezvous at Fort Union attracts avid modern frontiersmen who spend their days and nights just as the fur trappers did in the days when the post was the gateway to the riches of the West.

sent to Fort Yates, where he spent his last years on the Standing Rock Reservation. After Chief Joseph's surrender, Nez Perce prisoners were also brought here en route to Fort Leavenworth.

Abandoned in 1895, Fort Buford eventually became a state historic site. Its former officers headquarters now serves as a museum. Nearby are a cemetery, picnic area and hiking trails as well as a memorial to the Dakotas' first Masonic lodge, Yellowstone #88, active from 1871 to 1874.

The ghost town of **Mondak** straddles the border west of the forts. That location was not accidental: Montana was wet, North Dakota dry. Thus saloons chose the west side of the main thoroughfare, State Street, which coincided with the state line. Early in this century Mondak's population included hundreds of gamblers and the inhabitants of 15 houses of ill repute whose income flourished with rowdy parties of inebriated miners and ranch hands. Their enterprise was throttled by the Volstead Act of 1919, outlawing liquor all across the U.S. The town's tattered remains burned to the ground in 1928 except for two brick jails, a bank vault and the schoolhouse.

The Mondak ferry carried travelers across the rivers until 1913, when the Great Northern built lift-span bridges at **Snowden and Fairview, Mont**. (North Dakota's only railroad tunnel is 500 feet east of the Fairview bridge across the Yellowstone.) The center sections of both bridges could be hoisted up 300 feet to allow river navigation to pass beneath; that feature was used for the last time in 1935.

The bones of the outlaw Jesse Collins are said to be entombed in the concrete of Snowden Bridge, which was the last to be shared by railroads and automobiles until completion of the area's fifth bridge in 1985.

Two choices lie ahead: To make a shorter loop north and east to the Canadian border and the corner of the state, or to take the longer circuit around Lake Sakakawea south through the badlands and energy country, then back across the Fort Berthold Reservation. Perhaps you'll begin with the former, exploring the cities which most closely share Williston's history and influences on a Great Northern loop through North Dakota's first oil lands.

Like most political units in northwestern North Dakota, the name of **Epping** (104) reflects the Anglo-American background of the first residents of most of its town. It shares its name with a city in England. It's best known for Elmer Halvorson's Buffalo Trails Museum, which emphasizes the local history of Epping, **Spring Brook** (52) and **Wheelock** (34). Dioramas and room settings populated by persons made of chicken wire and plywood, newspapers and glue. Established in 1966.

Epping-Spring Brook Dam and its impoundment attract lots of attention in summer from anglers seeking walleye, bluegills and perch to avid waterskiers.

Wheelock (34) was named for Ralph Wheelock, an editorial writer for the Minneapolis Tribune. He thanked the town's founders by presenting them with the town pump.

Ray (766) in 1910 was one of the first American towns to adopt the city commission form of government. It hosts its annual Grain Palace Festival on the first full weekend of August.

Tioga (1,597) was named in 1902 for Tioga County, New York, home of its first residents. They were followed by a wave of Norwegian immigrants peppered with a handful of other ethnics, including a number of Japanese homesteaders (though only one of the latter proved up) who may have arrived with Great Northern Railroad construction crews. A metal sculpture of a Viking by Dean Bowman presides over the city park, while the story of settlement is told in the Norseman Museum.

North Dakota's first oil discovery was recorded by the Amerada Petroleum Company

Epping's frontier charm survives on its restored Main Street and the Buffalo Trails Museum.

at Clarence Iverson #1 on April 4, 1951, marked with a historic site six miles southwest of intersection of U.S. 2 and N.D. 40. Clarence and Thea Iverson received the first royalty payment ever in North Dakota — $172.27 for oil produced in April 1951. Two years later flames from flare pipes of more than 100 wells lit up the sky in the Tioga and Beaver Lodge oil fields. Signal Oil and Gas Company operates a natural gas processing plant.

The Williston Basin has estimated petroleum reserves of a billion barrels. Some 45,900,000 barrels were pumped in 1981, along with 70 billion cubic feet of recovered natural gas. Today North Dakota has a total of 3,343 oil wells and 57 natural gas wells.

Wildrose (214), named for the profusion of North Dakota's state flower flourishing in the area, was from 1911 to 1916 the largest primary grain market in the United States.

Tucked between **Corinth** and **Appam**, **Alamo** (122) shares both the tree and the Spanish name for the cottonwoods or poplars

Oil development no longer booms, but drilling continues in the Williston area where wells can be seen near city and farm alike. Oil still plays a dominant role in the economy of western North Dakota.

with that famous fort in Texas, whose restoration had been begun four years before the North Dakota city was incorporated in 1917.

North of Corinth, the Divide County seat of **Crosby** (1,469) was named for a partner in the land company which picked only the first of several townsites in 1903. The Soo Line came through one year later — and one mile east. Some rushed to that spot and called it Imperial. Two years after the founding it happened again with the Great Northern, which passed a mile in the opposite direction. Both the Soo and Imperial's population eventually yielded to Jim Hill, moving to a town platted in 1910 and officially renamed Crosby Revised.

The Divide County Historical Society moved fast to preserve its so-recent past in its outstanding Pioneer Village. Two dozen buildings preside over the site, along with a mammoth old Baukol-Noonan coal-mining shovel, antique cars and tractors. A threshing and Antique Show in July.

The Crosby area was the setting for "Northern Lights," John Hanson's acclaimed film on the hard times of 1915 that spawned the Nonpartisan League. Many local men and women played cameo roles. A winner of film awards at Cannes and other international festivals, the movie is occasionally screened in theatres around the area.

Among the Norwegian-American residents of **Noonan** (283) are a group whose roots are Belgian. Their roots go back to coal miners employed by the Truax Mine, the first lignite strip mine in North Dakota. It was named, though, for an Irishman, Patrick Noonan, whose family of nine sons homesteaded in the area. Town boomers once promoted it as "The White City", with lot contracts that specified that all buildings must be painted the color of snow.

Divide County shares with Williams the title as North Dakota's driest, with average rainfall of 13 inches or less. They also have

Crosby's Main Street is designed so that retail shops line the way to the Divide County Courthouse, which seems to dominate the center of town. An outstanding Pioneer Village hosts an annual threshing and anitque show in July.

one of the longer growing seasons, usually 130 days or more (compared to fewer than 110 in Cavalier County). Warm and dry as they are, perhaps it's no coincidence that this pair are the most thoroughly Norwegian of all in North Dakota.

Two contrasting comments on the area's terrain are reflected in the names of **Alkabo** (an accurate description combining the soil's "alkali" and "gumbo") and **Fortuna** (98), intended to mean "good fortune."

In his book "Blue Highways" William Least Heat Moon wrote of the area, "...the high moraine wheat fields took up the whole landscape. There was nothing else, except piles of stones like Viking burial mounds at the verges of tracts and big rock-pickers running steely fingers through the glacial soil to glean stone that freezes had heaved to the surface; behind the machines, the fields looked vacuumed. At a filling station, a man who long had farmed the moraine said the great ice sheets had only gone away to get

more rock. 'They'll be back. They always come back. What's to stop them?'"

Both Fortuna and **Ambrose** (60) are Canadian ports of entry.

Writing Rocks Historic Site on U.S. 85 between Alkabo and Grenora suggests that others may have had their little jokes as well. These two large rocks were incised in eons past by unknown people. The larger is five feet high and protected by a shelter on the site near where the glaciers deposited them in prehistory. The smaller rock found nearby spent 35 years at the University of North Dakota before its return to its companion's side. Indians knew the two as "Hoi-waukon" or Spirit Rocks. The late Indian expert Edward Milligan of Bottineau called them cup sculptures, with counterparts in the British Isles and western Europe; their inscriptions also resemble other mysterious rocks in Georgia, suggesting the people came from the southeast. Many Indian artifacts and tipi rings have been found in the immediate area.

Far from the beaten path is Writing Rock historic park, where hieroglyphics presumably carved by anicient Indians is displayed.

Hanks (10) owes its name to Powers Lake rancher and banker W.F. Hanks, who developed the townsite in 1916, the same year that **Grenora** (362) dates as its beginning. Its name reflects both towns' patron, the railroad: First letters of each word of "Great Northern Railway." It prospered as a major northwestern grain shipping point during the boom years of the late 'teens and '20s.

The Scandinavian heritage of much of northwestern North Dakota is celebrated each September in **Zahl** (34) with Samlingfest, or "festive gathering," an event which draws several thousand guests. Demonstrations of ethnic crafts — rosemaling, bobbin lace, Hardanger embroidery, wheat weaving — are a major attraction, along with traditional delicacies like lutefisk, lefse, sandbakkels, rommegrot, blodpolse and potet klub. The town is named after "Doc" Frederick Zahl, the famed buffalo hunter who out-shot Buffalo Bill Cody. Zahl, whose presence in the area dated back to the years just after the Civil War, established the largest cattle outfit along the Missouri.

Southbound out of Williston, U.S. Highway 85 carries travelers into McKenzie County to **Alexander** (358). Both were named in 1905 by Gov. E.Y. Sarles for infamous political boss Alexander McKenzie. The honor was no small thing: This county, North Dakota's largest, almost equals the combined area of Rhode Island and Delaware. The Lewis and Clark Trail Museum occupies the old Alexander schoolhouse. This is the home town of former U.S. congressman and governor Arthur A. Link. Among the area's original settlers were a dozen Negro families who homesteaded south of town between 1909 and 1915; all are gone today.

To the west, **Cartwright** was named for the area's first settler, the trapper and hunter George Cartwright, who with his sons operated big cattle ranches in the county from 1884 to 1900. **Charbonneau** shares its name with a nearby creek christened by Lewis and Clark in 1804 in honor of Sakakawea's halfbreed husband.

Past **Rawson** (12) and **Arnegard** (193) is **Watford City** (2,119), once called Banks for the lignite seams visible along a neighboring creek. In 1913 a local doctor renamed the settlement for his former home of Watford, Ontario. Watford City is the site of an annual June reunion of a group of veteran ranchers and cowhands called "50 Years in the Saddle," organized by Ceph Goddard of the neighboring VH Ranch. Art in the Park lends a different flavor each July. Shafer Jail, built five miles east of town of native stone, was the site on Jan. 29, 1931, of the last lynching in North Dakota. That night an angry mob stormed the jail, seized murderer Charles Bannon (who had confessed the slaying of six members of the Albert Haven family), and hanged him from a nearby bridge.

Among the area's more peaceful inhabitants was Jon Norstog, an immigrant farmer who wrote novels, poems, plays and theological tracts in a unique fusion of three Norwegian dialects. Norstog peddled his religious books from the back of his wagon to clergymen around the predominantly Norwegian-speaking counties of western North Dakota. He also edited two Norwegian-language newspapers published in the state and often contributed to a third.

The north unit of Theodore Roosevelt National Park lies south of Watford City. Its anguished rock and perversely peaceful vistas are considered more dramatic, more awe-inspiring and more challenging by most aficionados of the badlands. Its beauty is a reflection of its youth; glaciers carved its features eons later than the chiseling of the south unit of the park. Buffalo roam the sagebrush bottoms along with longhorn cattle, deer and elk, while the Little Missouri River knits its serpentine course between the buttes, pillars and rubble shaped by its waters native stone. In 1886 thieves stole Theodore Roosevelt's boat from his Elkhorn Ranch 25

The north unit of Theodore Roosevelt National Park is thought by many to be the most beautiful and is dominated by the Little Missouri River and a tall line of rugged buttes.

miles to the south. Roosevelt pursued them through the area encompassed by the park. Capturing them at the mouth of Cherry Creek, he sternly marched them 60 miles overland to Dickinson to stand trial.

The park offers 36 miles of scenic roads along with an extensive network of hiking and horse trails. Rangers are on duty to preserve the pristine park from its visitors and the visitors from the park: Back-country hikers are required to register their routes and approximate schedules with the park officers so that they can be found if they should run into trouble. Tales abound of even experienced parties becoming lost and disoriented in the crazy and unforgiving landscape.

Grassy Butte shares its locale with the jutting landform from which it draws its name, the area's only mesa that's not severely bald. The Grassy Butte Post Office, which served area farm families from 1914 to 1964, is now maintained as a historic site. It's built of cedar logs, mud and sod with grass growing on its roof. In that 50-year span only two postmasters, Donald McKenzie and James Warren, cancelled stamps and sorted letters in its adobe splendor. Several natural gas processing plants are operated in the vicinity of Grassy Butte, Killdeer, Alexander, Cartwright and Arnegard.

Killdeer (790) is east into Dunn County along U.S. Highway 200. An NDRA rodeo is held each year in mid-August. The town borrows its name from the Killdeer Mountains, actually a pair of high flat-topped ridges with fluted edges shaped by water, wind and time. The mountains consist of hard sedimented volcanic ash that settled to the bottom of a prehistoric lake when the Rockies were young and explosive. The slopes are forested on the shady north with oak, aspen and birch, while their inhospitable southern flanks are dotted with cacti, yucca and tough prairie wildflowers.

The path to the Medicine Hole is steep and the climb is exhausting, but once on top, the Killdeer Mountains offer a breathtaking view of western North Dakota and the battlefield below.

The Killdeers' name comes from the Sioux, who called area "Tah-kah-o-kuty," or "place where they kill the deer," they were preceded by others in the mists of time. Archeologists have observed a number of mysterious medicine wheels, large circles of stones marked off with spokes that may be 5,000 years old, interspersed with more familiar and far more recent tipi rings.

That aura of mystery extends to the fissure called Medicine Hole, one of North Dakota's few caves. Smokey fog rises from its mouth on cold mornings; it exhales its chill breath all summer along. Uncertain humans have dynamited it twice in the twentieth century — once to close it to keep away the curious, then again to reopen it on their behalf. Indian legend identifies it as the abyss from which the first people and animals stepped forth from the heart of the planet in the beginning of time, or from which the first buffalo emerged onto the plains.

Led by General Alfred Sully, 3,000 troops attacked a large encampment here in 1864 during the campaign to punish the Sioux for the bloody Minnesota uprising of 1862. They killed many of the Hunkpapa, Sans Arc, Blackfeet, Miniconjou, Yanktonai and Santee men, women and children. The survivors fled to Killdeer Mountain and badlands; legend has it that some escaped into Medicine Hole. After the battle, the soldiers destroyed an estimated 200 tons of buffalo meat the Indians had been stockpiling for winter provisions. Killdeer Mountain Historic Site marks graves of two soldiers killed here; the battlefield itself is open to the public.

Little Missouri State Park 17 miles north of Killdeer includes more than 5,900 wild and undeveloped wilderness acres above the

500-foot-deep valley of the Little Missouri (now submerged by the reservoir). The area supports mule deer, coyotes and bobcats, as well as golden and bald eagles and prairie falcons. Rent a horse (and perhaps the services of a guide), and ride or hike on 75 miles of rugged trails.

Lost Bridge on N.D. Highway 22 coincides with the old trail crossing of Little Missouri used in the late 1800s by cattle and horse ranchers herding stock from Killdeer Mountain ranches to winter camps on fertile river bottoms. The highway bridge was completed in October 1931 but stood almost unused for 25 years, since no decent roads connected at either end; it served merely as a shortcut for area cattlemen who otherwise had to drive herds west to Watford City to cross river on Long X Bridge. Finally with the advent of Garrison Dam and Reservoir roads were graded to both sides in 1953. The road to the north was paved in 1963, and the south in 1967.

Winding its way through open range and rugged country, Highway 22 is one of the most scenic roads in North Dakota.

East of Killdeer is Lake Ilo, a manmade impoundment built in 1939 by Works Progress Administration. It's surrounded by a lush 5000-acre wildlife refuge with bright prospects for bird-watching, nature photography, fishing and picnics. The state's record carp — a 36-inch-plus hog weighing 26 lb. 10 oz. — was caught here in 1988.

Dunn Center (170) and the same-named county were christened by territorial legislator E.A. Williams for his close friend John P. Dunn, one of Bismarck's first mayors. Beef from this ranching area is the principle

ingredient of C&I Jerky, an all-beef snack with no sugar or fillers. Other local attractions include the Dunn County Historical Museum and Slater's Resort on Lake Sakakawea, which offers cabins, campsites, boat rentals, food, gas, bait and other services necessary to permit boatless anglers to take advantage of the big lake's reputation for lunkers. It's headquarters for a walleye derby and the Badlands Regatta in June.

Other Dunn County towns include **Werner** and **New Hradec**, which was settled by Czechoslovakians or Bohemians from the Crimea in 1887.

Despite their names bespeaking the Wild West, **Halliday** (355), **Dodge** (199) and **Marshall** were named respectively for a postmaster, a banker and a North Dakota congressman. Marshall's most famous native is rodeo star Brad Gjermundson, four-time holder of the world saddle bronc championship. Wide vistas of ripening wheat gave Mercer County's **Golden Valley** (377) its name.

The unique name of **Zap** (625), a town which dates back only to 1917, attracted its most recent brush with fame. In 1968 college students from a four-state area (following the suggestion of *The Spectrum*, North Dakota State University's student newspaper) converged on the small town by the thousands for a weekend revel that ultimately bore very little resemblance to Woodstock. Suggested only in fun, the invasion turned into trouble when the number of visitors overwhelmed the town's hospitality. The National Guard was called out to keep the peace; the crowd became rowdy, and Zap residents still complain about the damage and concern they caused. North American Coal's Indian Head Mine here

Landscapes in Dunn, Mercer and Oliver counties still show the natural prairie and the hardy grasses and flowers which grow on the rocky slopes.

supplies United Power Association's Stanton Station.

This is energy country. North Dakota ranks 12th among U.S. states coal-producing states and seventh in combined production of coal, oil and energy, which amount in turn to 17 percent of the state's economic base. Seven of North Dakota's 11 licensed lignite mines are operated in the immediate area, accounting for more than 90 percent of the state's total production. They're carving away at deposits believed to be world's largest, with some 35 billion recoverable tons. Nearly 28 million tons were mined in 1988 by companies employing 3,800 workers at an annual payroll of $126 million.

Beulah (5,612) is the site of two gargantuan projects based on that coal — Basin Electric Power Cooperative's 900-megawatt Antelope Valley Station and the multi-billion-dollar Great Plains Coal Gasification Project, as well as Coyote Station (which went on-line in 1979). Antelope Valley's two units (on-line in 1984 and 1986) supply power to 118 rural power cooperatives serving 1.2 million consumers in eight states. It's powered by lignite from Coteau Properties' Freedom Mine to the north (by far the largest lignite mining operation in the state) and Knife River Coal's Beulah Mine south of town.

Basin itself dates back to 1961, when engineers realized that hydroelectric power from Garrison and other dams could no longer supply area's needs. Coal-fired electrical generation plants became one answer, with Governor Bill Guy urging development of those facilities close to the lignite mines that fueled them. The cooperative purchased the Great Plains gasification plant in 1988 after it failed to meet the projections of the consortium of midwestern utilities originally formed to build it with federally guaranteed loans. Born during Jimmy Carter's presidency in response to the energy crisis of the 1970s, the project was designed to manufacture synthetic gas from lignite coal. When

The area around Beulah and Hazen is Coal Country, where coal is mined and electricity or synthetic natural gas is produced by innovative and highly technological methods. Visitors may tour the plants and mines.

petroleum prices plummeted in the 1980s, its synthetic fuels were left high and dry, uncompetitive in the marketplace.

Beulah's Mercer County Historical Museum is open weekend afternoons in summer. A popular local souvenir is jewelry, spoons and other collectibles made of coal dust. The town also hosts the Mercer County Fair and the Cowboys Reunion Rodeo in mid-August. The archeological site called the Crowley Flint Quarry is south of town, though almost impossible to find without a guide; it was the

source of flint used by Indians for knives, arrowheads, tools and utensils.

Near Beulah is Dakota Waters Resort, Sakakawea's newest, with a lodge and store of native logs harvested in the southern badlands. Operated by the Hanson family (which also hosts guests at the Logging Camp Ranch near Amidon), the development includes a campground, marina and other amenities.

Hazen (3,352), named for the third assistant U.S. postmaster general back in

A new interpretative center will soon be built on the site.

This National Historic Site is rich in artifacts and the history of the "People of the Pheasants", who were agriculturalists for thousands of years before smallpox decimated their numbers.

1884, has become noted for more illustrious accomplishments today. Along with Beulah, it's the capital of North Dakota's energy country. Rapid growth followed the development of the region's mine-head power plants in the 1970s, straining but not breaking the cities' traditional way of life. The Hazen school at the time became a national leader in innovative methods.

Lewis and Clark noted a Mandan village called Mah-har-ha located where **Stanton** (801), the Mercer County seat, now stands. They used lignite from the area to fire the expedition blacksmith's forge. The area's first large lignite-fired generating plant, the Leland Olds Station, began operation in 1966, followed by a plant built by the United Power Association in 1967 and Leland Olds Unit 2 in 1975. They're supplied with lignite from the adjoining Glenharold Mine.

The entire area's heavily German-Russian heritage is reflected in locally popular dishes like knoepfle soup (with heavy noodle-like dumplings) and fleischkeuchle, a fried pie filled with meat, potatoes and onion similar to a Welsh pastie. Golden Fleischkeuchle of Stanton manufactures the frozen pastries for sale throughout the region.

South of Stanton on N.D. 48 is **Center** (900), which does in fact stand at the center of Oliver County and naturally serves as its seat of government. A memorial on the courthouse grounds recounts a tale from the two-day March blizzard of 1920. Hazel Miner and her younger brother and sister left school in a sleigh, which overturned in a waterhole. Hazel worked for hours trying the free the horse but failed. She covered her brother and sister with the blankets and with her own wraps and lay on top of them to keep them warm. When they were found, the two younger children were cold and hungry, but Hazel had frozen to death.

Minnkota Power operates the Milton Young Station not far from Center, fired by lignite from the Baukol-Noonan strip mine. Water used to cool the plants' stacks is circulated in Nelson Lake, a four-star fishing spot featuring the finest largemouth bass fishing in North Dakota. The state record largemouth (8 lbs. 1.5 oz.) was taken here in 1982, along with the all-time whopper crappie (3 lbs. 1 oz.) in 1981. Since the warm water prevents the lake from freezing, it offers a bizarre site in January and February, when hardy anglers work its steaming waters from their boats.

The Knife River Indian Villages north of Stanton are tied to the story of Lewis and Clark and Fort Mandan Historic Site east of Missouri. Designated a national historic site in the 1970s, the preserve encompasses the site of villages originally occupied by Mandans (later Hidatsa and Arikara) as early as 1000 A.D.

The Mandan, who called themselves "People of the Pheasants," are considered perhaps one of oldest agricultural tribes in North America. An early white visitor called them "most interesting, friendly and gentlemanly of the Western Indians." The peaceful agricultural tribes tended extensive gardens along the river, and brokered much trading among the nomadic plains tribes. In 1800 these earth-lodge villages' combined population was substantially more than that shown by the 1980 census along the entire stretch of the Missouri within North Dakota.

Here Lewis and Clark were introduced to Sakakawea during the winter of 1804-1805, which they spent at Fort Mandan east of the river. The teenage mother, who'd been won in a dice game by her disreputable French-Indian husband Charbonneau, carried her newborn son Pomp along with the expedition as she guided the explorers safely west through lands of the Shoshone. North Dakota stands alone in spelling her name with the letter "k," but with good reason: "Sakakawea" is the Hidatsa word for Bird Woman, considered the meaning of her name ("tsakaka" or bird, and "wia" for woman). The more common spelling "Sacajawea" is Shoshone for "boat launcher."

The national historic site hosts Fur Trade Days in July; a Lewis and Clark reenactment in early August, and a pow wow in September. Locally made Indian crafts are available at the Visitors Center, which is open daily year round. Trails accommodate hiking and cross-country skiing. The site's long-range plan includes a major interpretive center, theatre, museum, archeological research and area for storage of countless artifacts collected on University of North Dakota expeditions led by Dr. Stan Ahler, who's documenting sites up and down the river.

Fort Clark Historic Site to the south commemorates the American Fur Company post which ranked second only to Fort Union. Built 1829 by James Kipp, it was named for William Clark of expeditionary fame. But its most horrible significance was lent by smallpox, which arrived here on a steamboat from St. Louis in 1837. During the next eight years it raged among the Indians, killing 95 percent of the Mandans and thousands of Hidatsa and Arikara; the mobile Sioux were struck, but far less severely. Fort Clark itself

A variety of activities takes place on the grounds where Sakakawea once lived, from canoeing the Knife River in spring, fur trade weekends in summer and skiing in the winter.

was closed for a time during the pandemic and later abandoned.

Opening in 1989, Cross Ranch State Park five miles southeast of **Hensler** preserves a slice of the state's natural heritage. The rapidly developing project calls for primitive camping and picnicking, fishing and boating access along one of the last free-flowing and undeveloped stretches of Missouri Winter, along with cross-country skiing and snowshoeing in winter.

Its trails connect to Cross Ranch Nature Preserve, almost 6,000 acres owned by The Nature Conservancy of native prairie, woody draws and riverbottom forest. The preserve is rich in wildlife including deer, owls, hawks, turkeys, eagles and songbirds, as well as a reestablished bison herd. Archeological surveys have uncovered artifacts originating from 6000 B.C. to 1 A.D., as well as those of more recent Mandan and Hidatsa cultures — village sites, burial grounds, effigies, buffalo killing grounds and eagle trapping pits.

The park and preserve are part of ranch established 1897 by A.D. Gaines who acquired Theodore Roosevelt's Maltese Cross brand and named his ranch after it. The area, subsequently owned by Bob Levis, was purchased by the Conservancy with more than $1.5 million donated by 6,500 individuals, foundations and corporations.

The North Dakota Game and Fish Department preserves Smith Grove four miles south of ranch headquarters, one of the state's most impressive forests. Twelve of its cottonwoods are more than 15 feet in circumference and up to 100 feet tall, with estimated ages of from 250 to 300 years old. The area is home to deer and wild turkeys restocked by area sportsmen beginning in the 1950s.

The Cross Ranch offers hikers the choice of river woodlands or natural prairie. A new state park is being developed and the state's Centennial buffalo herd grazes peacefully in a nearby pasture.

Pick City (264) heralds the coming of Garrison Dam along N.D. Highway 1806, a magnet for fishermen, campers and boaters from throughout the region. The little town buzzes with life during the summer, thanks the traffic of hopeful fishermen... especially those after salmon each fall. Boat charters and guides are available here, along with supplies and bait.

The entrance to Lake Sakakawea State Park is just past town. Popular with local campers and anglers as well as those from farther afield who spend vacations in the area, the park offers a full range of services, including a marina, boat rentals and gas, fully modern RV campsites and Rent-a-Camp tent facilities, picnicking and playgrounds, an amphitheatre for ranger programs and two large boat ramps. Blessed with the steady winds shared by all of North Dakota, the park hosts several big events including the North American Regatta, which began in 1986; the North American Hobie Championships, to start in '89; and a salmon fishing derby in August. Windsurfers, Hobies and classy sailboats dot the waters, but overall, fishing remains Number One. While walleyes still reign as the angler's premier prey, those equipped with down-riggers are passionate about the flourishing population of chinook salmon. Winter sports enthusiasts enjoy snowmobile trails and ice fishing.

The long dark silhouette of Garrison Dam lies southeast of the park, its towering hydroelectric unit's rather low profile appearing like the tip of an iceberg. (From the top to their underwater foundations, it's nine stories tall.) A 100-square-foot mural of Sakakawea painted by Hidatsa artist Clarence Cuts the Rope is displayed in the lobby of the power plant, which is open to tours throughout the summer.

Some of the area's best farmland was inundated in the 1950s by this dam and its 200-mile-long reservoir, at some points 14 miles wide. Garrison is one of six in the Pick-

Below Garrison Dam the Missouri River offers many recreational possibilities, from fishing and boating, to hiking and picnicking. The tailrace annually produces whopper-sized northerns, walleye, and salmon.

The sandly beaches of the Missouri River are great places for family outings. The "northern hole" a few miles below the dam is a favorite for children who swim in the warm pools left by the fluctuating river levels.

Lake Sakakawea is one of North Dakota's premier summer recreation areas, and with over 1,400-miles of shoreline, sailing has become very popular. The large campgrounds, both on the river or above the dam on the lake, are usually filled every weekend.

Built by the Corps of Engineers in the late 1940s to house the workers building Garrison Dam, Riverdale is a neatly planned community which officially became an independent city on July 26, 1986.

Sloan Plan for development of the Missouri Basin, primarily for downstream flood control but also for irrigation, hydroelectric power and recreation. Begun in 1947, the dam finally was closed in 1953; earthwork was completed in 1954. The last of five power generators went on-line in 1960. The dam — considered the largest rolled earth-fill dam in the world—was built at a cost of $294 million.

There's exceptional fishing at the tailrace, from which anglers have pulled more than a dozen state record fish — brown and rainbow trout, coho and chinook salmon and whitefish. Visitors can usually see fishing boats drifting in the current, rods bobbing above and jigging (mainly for walleyes) below. The stretch of fast water also yields large rainbow and brown trout and carp.

Garrison Dam National Fish Hatchery below the dam was established to support, among other species, the lake's growing chinook salmon fishery. It stocks from one to one and one-half million chinook fingerlings each year. Above the dam, wildlife biologists from the University of North Dakota study

waterfowl in the living laboratory provided by Mallard Island, the top of a hill left high and dry above the lake's waters. Now birds breed there in enviable peace, safe from most landlocked predators.

Riverdale got its start in the 1940s as a bedroom community for construction workers building Garrison Dam under direction of the U.S. Corps of Engineers. Its peak population was more than 4,000; today it sports 279 permanent residents, who in 1985 received title to land until then owned by the Corps. It acquired its melodious name in a contest sponsored by 24 North Dakota newspapers in 1946. The winning entry (of a total of 20,000) was credited to Mrs. T.O. Lervick of Granville, whose prize was $24 in cash (one buck from each newspaper).

Riverdale is now proclaimed the home of Misty the Mermaid, a distinctly modern twist on the legends of the lake. Here's how it's told: "Legend has it that Misty the Mermaid and her lover swam the lengths of the Missouri River since dawn of time. He possessed great strength and she, great magical power. In a

whisper of time, a great barrier was built and for reasons unknown, the lovers were separated. She now remains locked in the mighty depths of Lake Sakakawea reigning and controlling the destiny of her waters and all creatures that abound."

Coleharbor (150) is the headquarters of Audubon National Wildlife Refuge. The refuge covers the south half and shore of Lake Audubon. Totten Trail Park on the north shore offers fishing and camping facilities. The first local settlement, Coal Harbor, reflected the area's lignite deposits which peaked out from the nearby banks of a boat landing on the Missouri. Though the site was shifted east of the original town in 1904 by the Soo Line, the railroad kept the original name — with one revision. Its spelling was changed to Coleharbor to incorporate a simultaneous reference to employee W.A. Cole.

Travelers on U.S. 83 cross the dividing point between Lakes Sakakawea and Audubon on the two-mile-long Snake Creek Embankment. At its northern end is the Snake Creek

Pumping Station, a key feature of the Garrison Diversion irrigation project. The Custer Game Management Area just northwest of the bridge encompasses the spot where the Falkirk Mining Company has reclaimed its lignite-mining spoil banks as a hilly, brush-covered haven for wildlife.

The town of **Garrison** (1,830) is home of real fish stories — the feats of native anglers commemorated in the North Dakota Fishing Hall of Fame, and one Wally the Walleye, a 35-footer who towers over the park at the end of Main Street. (Oddly enough, Wally has a twin named Willy the Walleye, who inspires fishermen in, of all places, Garrison, Minn. Neither town — or fish — was aware of the other when it acquired its monumental trophy, apparently thanks to an overeager but underimaginative fiberglass salesman.)

South of town, Fort Stevenson State Park bears the name of the army garrison that once stood nearby but was immersed below the surface of the lake. The park boasts a full-service marina with concessions and rentals of fishing, sailing and houseboats. Two boat ramps permit launching of private craft. The grounds also include modern and primitive campsites, picnic facilities, a restaurant, a prairie dog town, and the opportunity to Rent-a-Camp, complete with tent, table and firewood, from the North Dakota Park Service. The Garrison Cup Sailboat Race is held here in June, followed by the DeTrobriand Bay Whirlwind Sailboard Race in July and the North Dakota Governors Cup Walleye Fishing Derby in July.

While walleyes are still prized, other Sakakawea fishing includes salmon, trout, bass and northerns. It was once a national hotspot for northern pike in its first years; the state record 37-plus northern was caught here in 1968. But as the lake has evolved, breeding conditions necessarily changed. Today big northerns are highly unusual.

Another spot to launch an assault on fish is at Indian Hills Recreation Area on Good

Garrison is the home of the Governor's Cup walleye fishing tournament held each July and drawing fishing teams and spectators from several states. Charter boats and guides now work the big lake primarily for salmon, but also for the tasty but wily walleye.

Bear Bay 34 miles southwest of Garrison. It's jointly operated by the state parks department and the Three Affiliated Tribes, and offers semi-modern campsites on a bluff overlooking the lake, a complex of four modern cabins, and both boat rentals and fishing guides to take advantage of excellent walleye fishing.

At **White Shield**, west of **Emmet** on N.D. 1804, white monuments mark the graves of some 100 Arikara veterans of the U.S. Armed Services. Buried here at Indian Scout Cemetery No. 1 are three scouts who died with General George Custer's command, whose graves were moved here from Like-a-Fishhook Village, as well as soldiers, sailors, airmen and marines who served their country from the Little Big Horn to Vietnam.

Roseglen was the home of the late George Albrecht, widely known as "Skywolf." From 1926 through 1949 he aided North Dakota

ranchers by gunning down 3,363 coyotes — from the air. Then considered a threat to livestock, coyotes were hunted throughout the period for a bounty. Albrecht and partner Nick Reuter mainly hunted the Missouri River corridor but also ventured into the badlands; they were considered the "world champion aerial coyote exterminators." Albrecht is also remembered for flying his World War I vintage J.I. Standard airplane under the Elbowoods bridge at its dedication in 1934 and for flying notorious Wild Bill Langer on his whirlwind gubernatorial campaign trips. Nearby Raub is the home of Myers' Meats and Specialties, a butchering plant that produces regionally popular jerky, sausages and German burgers.

North on N.D. 28 past the Soo Line town of **Ryder** (158), **Makoti** (199) hosts one of North Dakota's largest threshing shows early in October. It's an alternate spelling of "maakoti," the Mandan word for the largest

of their villages. Hiddenwood Lake National Wildlife Refuge south of town offers fishing as well as waterfowl-watching. **Plaza** (222) really does have a central park plaza, around which other businesses and homes were arranged during settlement days in the first decade of the 20th century.

Named for the driver of the area's first mail stage, **Parshall** (1,059) is the site of the unusual Paul Broste Rock Museum. Situated in a castle-like building of fieldstone, it displays the mineral collection of the late poet, artist, philosopher and rockhound. Two spiral "trees" of various rocks polished to spherical precision are among its highlights.

These towns, along with New Town and Mandaree, are on the Fort Berthold Indian Reservation, now home to white families as well as members of the Three Affiliated Tribes — the Mandan, Hidatsa and Arikara. In 1980 North Dakota's total Indian population of about 20,000 represented about three percent

of the state's population of 653,000, with the number of Indian people almost double that of 1960.

New Town (1,335) is literally a "new town," established after Garrison Reservoir inundated Sanish three miles to the west, Van Hook seven miles east, and Elbowoods 30 miles south, all officially abandoned in September 1954. The ground-breaking ceremony was held in September 1950 on high ground. The Corps of Engineers platted the New Town townsite, and the federal government built its streets, curbs and seven miles of sidewalks. The Northrup Corporation now operates a manufacturing plant here which builds electronic hardware and complete diagnostic systems for the Navy and Air Force.

Crow Flies High Butte west of city overlooking lake honors the famed Hidatsa chief who established a village northwest of site. Keelboats and mackinaw boats frequently traveled the river far below in fur trading days, followed by steamboats which supplied fur posts, military forts and mining operations. An odd cowboy statue of Earl Bunyan, the overlooked cowboy brother of lumberjack Paul, stands just outside of town. It was the creation of the late Fred Larocque, a New Town cowboy, saloon owner and storyteller who "discovered" this forgotten Bunyan who wandered the Missouri River valley, imprinting the land with his big boots from Williston to Elbowoods.

The mile-long Four Bears Memorial Bridge spans a narrow spot on the reservoir west of New Town. It incorporates three truss spans from the bridge that once crossed the river at Elbowoods, freighted here by flatbed truck and welded into the center of the present bridge. (Another handy bridge, the one at Sanish, suffered a worse fate: It was sold for salvage.)

In its name, the contemporary bridge carries on a solution worked out when the former structure was christened in 1933. The

Rows of white markers in the Indian Scout Cemetery near White Shield mark the burial sites of some one hundred Arikara men who are veterans of armed conflicts. Three of Custer's scouts from the Little Big Horn are also buried here.

On the upper reaches of the 200-mile long Lake Sakakawea, New Town was created as a home for residents of three Indian villages inundated by the big waters. Houseboating to remote bays is popular after the vessels pass under the Four Bears Bridge, a historic, narrow, yet imposing structure which is a vital transportation link.

Mandans wanted to name it for their Four Bears, subject of many paintings by Carl Bodmer and George Catlin a century before. The Hidatsas wanted it named after their Four Bears, who'd died several years earlier. Thus the southern end was named for the Mandan and the northern for the Hidatsa; while the new bridge runs east and west, the same arrangement applies. Seventeen other leaders were added to its official designation as a sort of subtitle. For the Mandans: Charging Eagle, Red Buffalo Cow, Flying Eagle, Black Eagle and Waterchief. For the Hidatsa: Poor Wolf, Porcupine, Crow Paunch, Big Brace, Crow Flies High, Big Hawk and Old Dog. And for the Arikara, third of the Three Affiliated Tribes: Bear Chief, Son of the Star, White Shield, Peter Beauchamp Sr. and Bobtail Bull. All in all, the bridge sports a unique distinction. It may be the only one in the U.S. whose crossing is shorter than its name.

The Three Affiliated Tribes maintain a recreation area at Four Bears Resort west of the city, as well as several others around the lake. Their museum displays artifacts from throughout the reservation and sells locally made arts and crafts. The Native American Art Display & Auction is held in August in connection with the Little Shell Pow Wow.

Lake Sakakawea functionally split the reservation in two at the same time it submerged well-established villages, covered farms on the fertile bottoms and disrupted reservation residents' self-sufficient way of life. The unofficial capital of its southwestern reaches is **Mandaree**, west on N.D. 23 and then south on N.D. 22. The modern village was established by the federal government in 1945 to relocate residents from the fertile river bottoms to be flooded by Garrison Dam. Its location was chosen not for natural beauty or function, but because it's roughly in the center of the western section of the reservation. |||

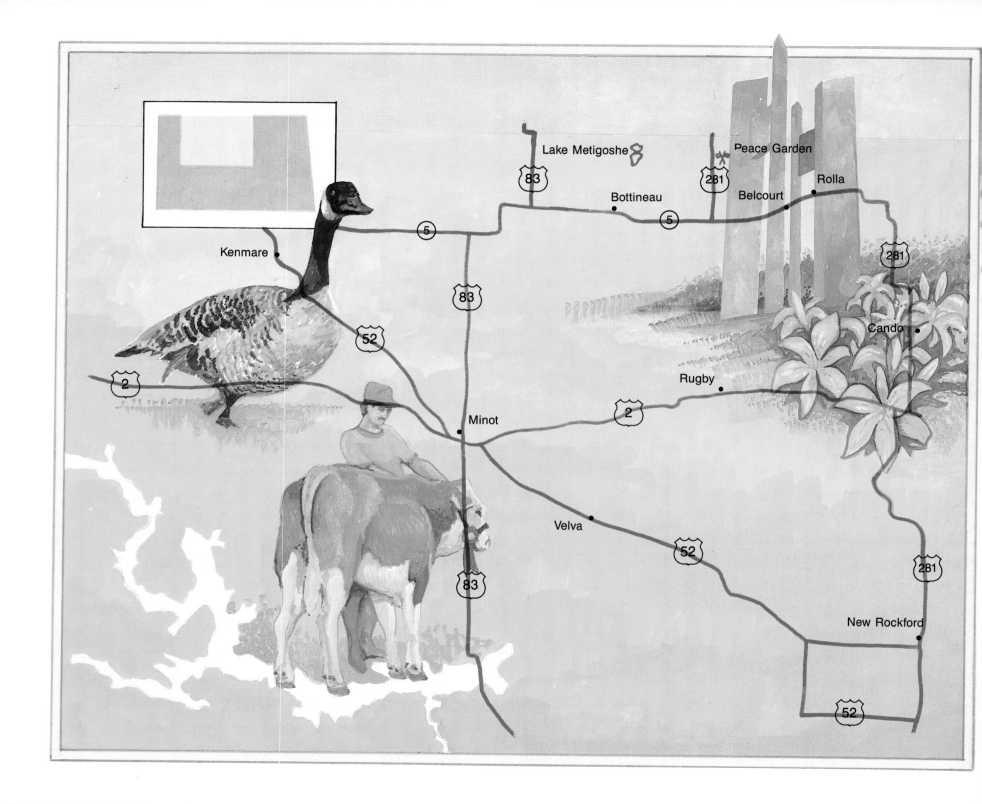

Lake Metigoshe

83

Bottineau

281 Peace Garden

Belcourt

Rolla

5

5

Kenmare

83

281

52

Cando

2

Rugby

2

Minot

Velva

52

52

83

New Rockford

281

52

The Peaceful Border Lands

The highlights: The international boundary of Canada and the United States slices neatly through the heart of the continent. Here a melting pot of people from many nations have carved out neat farms, sprawling ranches and lakeland retreats with attractions ranging from the North Dakota State Fair at Minot to the world-famous International Peace Garden.

The route: Starting at Minot, direct your travels north via U.S. Highway 52 to Kenmare then east on N.D. 5 toward Bottineau and Belcourt. Turn south on U.S. 281 to reach Cando. Complete the loop to Minot on U.S. Highway 2; or continue on U.S. 281 to New Rockford, then cross over to U.S. 52 for the last leg of the tour.

Why not **Minot**? That's the rhetorical question that's been asked in this city of 32,843 since its wild west beginnings as a principle destination on James J. Hill's fast-moving Great Northern Railroad...raw, rugged and vivid. In the earliest days of 1887, the Great Northern conductor would announce, "Minot, M-I-N-O-T. Prepare to meet your God."

Named for Henry D. Minot, a college friend of Theodore Roosevelt, the city sits in the shade of cottonwoods along the Souris (or Mouse) River — pleasant and friendly along its 10-odd winding miles for much of the year, but given to headline-grabbing rages during the spring thaw. Then it rushes south from Canada, changes its mind and splashes north again. Both river and city occupy the fertile bed of glacial Lake Souris, which like larger Lake Agassiz in the Red River Valley bequeathed smooth rich soil and level fields. Thanks to the receding glacier, that horizontal sweep is broken up by the Turtle Mountains, a region of nicely sloping landscapes furred with natural forest and set with gem-like, loon-dotted lakes. Minot's service area of north central North Dakota has something in common with every other corner of the state. Its farms parallel the tidy fields and straight-line furrows of Red River Valley agriculture. It shares southwestern North Dakota's ranching history; large cattle ranches still dominate parts of the region along with tidy grain farms and mixed crop-and-

livestock enterprises. Like the northeastern quarter, its history is alive with explorers, fur traders, Indians and Metis buffalo hunts. It sits on the eastern rim of the Williston Basin, with its deep riches of petroleum and lignite coal. And along with the south central section, its pothole-strewn prairie welcomes millions of ducks, geese, long-legged waterbirds and musical songbirds in their fall and spring migrations. The site of the city was selected by happenstance. Hill's railroad builders paused near here to bridge Gassman Coulee in their 1886 push west from Devils Lake. A tent city blossomed overnight; it was transplanted instantly to the banks of the Souris when the railroad's townsite was revealed. The perennial nickname of Magic City was earned during that first season, when its population zoomed from none to 5,000.

Among them were inhabitants typical of unrefined western settlements — transient railroad gangs, saloon-keepers and shady ladies, horse and cattle rustlers, and a sprinkling of criminals who'd eluded the law and slipped across the border from Canada. That character was not only endured but flaunted; the first newspaper in fact was called the Minot Rustler-Tribune.

Souris River ranches date from the 1880s, with widespread farming coming relatively late when so-called Imperial Ward County was opened to homesteading in 1896. In 1905 Minot recorded the largest number of land entries of all the land offices in the nation. That mega-county was split into the present counties of Renville, Burke, Mountrail and Ward in 1910.

The arrival of the Soo Line in 1893 and the advent of the state's first regular bus transportation (from Minot to Bismarck in 1922) helped cement Minot's position as the major distribution, medical and educational center for northwestern and north central North Dakota.

As is fitting for a transportation hub, the state's first aeroplane was flown here by Dewey Dorman in 1908. Ordered by mail, it arrived at the Minot depot and was hauled home on a dray just in time for the flying exhibition he'd agreed to perform for the Ward County Fair.

Wind grounded Dorman on day one. On the second, after several attempts, he soared a full four feet above the ground. Later in the show, the plane caught fire; Dorman and friends were forced to put it out in the Souris River. Not counting Dorman's feat, one of the state's first successful flying exhibitions was staged soon after by Lucky Bob St. Henry in his craft called "Sweetheart."

Minot's most prominent historic structures include the 1912 Soo Line depot now renovated as office space, which is entered on the National Register of Historic Places. Other landmark buildings (among them, the Second National Bank Building) are the work of architect Robert B. Stacy-Judd, who came to Minot from England in 1914 and later went on to prominence in western Canada and Los Angeles.

Two major institutions draw people to Minot — Minot State University and Minot Air Force Base, located immediately north of the city. The latter is the home of the 91st Strategic Missile Wing, 5th Bombardment Wing and the 5th Fighter Interceptor Squadron, with 6,093 active duty members and 7,600 dependents. It hosts the public at Northern Neighbors Day in August.

The university stands partly on land donated by Minot's first settler, Erik Ramstad, who said of his early days, "It was a wilderness: no preachers, no doctors, no neighbors, nothing; but we came out all right." Authorized by amendment to the state constitution, it was one of the last state educational institutions to be established, opening its doors as a normal school in 1913. (Only Dickinson State College, which began classes in 1918, is of more recent vintage.) Today the college boasts a domed stadium for sports and other events.

The oldest zoo in North Dakota was established in 1915 in Roosevelt Park with two dozen fox and grey squirrels, followed in the 1920s by two Nubian lions. Now it cares for some 51 species of animals, from lions,

Although born as a rowdy railroad tent city, Minot today is a well-ordered, thriving service-center hub for northwestern North Dakota. An Air Force Base and state university have contributed to Minot's status as a growing, active city.

jaguars and Bengal tigers to cougars, waterfowl (including seasonal drop-ins from region's refuges), Bactrian camels, zebras, peacocks, a wallaby, llamas, apes plus a variety of monkeys. Children are welcome to get acquainted firsthand in the petting zoo.

The North Dakota State Fair hosts as many as 300,000 visitors during its week-long run in late July. Like all exponents of the great midwestern rural tradition, it features a crazy quilt of contests, shows and attractions, from school, 4-H and FFA livestock, agriculture and home economics exhibits to the North Dakota Rodeo Association's state finals championship rodeo; from an antique tractor pull to what's officially designated as the North Dakota State Parade; from auto races to dueling tractors and monster trucks; and

from big-name grandstand entertainment to a carnival midway blasted by neon and pulsing rock music late into the night. The fair also offers a week's worth of livestock shows — from swine, cattle, sheep and horses to rabbits and goats. There are said to be 28,000 competitive exhibits (for a total of nearly $200,000 in premiums) and 660 commercial displays.

The State Fairgrounds is also the home of the Ward County Historical Museum, with its village of authentic homes and establishments from the pioneer era, as well as the Minot Art Gallery, the Minot Curling Rink and the All Seasons Arena, where sports and entertainment are scheduled year-round.

Major Minot events include Norsk Hostfest in October. With world-class American and

Rural North Dakota congregates in the July heat for the annual State Fair at Minot, finding attractions both traditonal and contemporary - from livestock shows, rodeos and competitions for everything from flower-raising to quilting, to the giant midway lighting up the summer night.

Gassman Coulee west of Minot presented Great Northern engineers with a major hurdle to cross, and in the process, led to the formation of the city.

Norwegian entertainers, ethnic foods, dancing and crafts, it's considered the premier Norwegian festival in Upper Midwest. It's been featured in major Norwegian magazines as an example of keeping Old World traditions alive in the New World. The event's founder, state senator and former mayor Chester Reitan, has been awarded Norway's St. Olaf medal for his city's work in preserving culture.

Other festivals include Pastaville USA in November and Winterfest in January and February. The first acknowledges that North Dakota farmers produce 85 percent of America's durum wheat, the principle ingredient of quality pasta. Among its highlights is the Mr. Spaghetti contest, with contestants judged on how much their legs resemble spaghetti — that is, skinny and pale. The latter makes the best of winter with the

Minot to Regina International 250 snowmobile cross-country race, the longest true cross country stock snowmobile adventure in North America. The schedule is filled out with an ethnic food fest, a children's carnival and winter sports competitions (indoors and out) in every conceivable pastime.

Among notable Minot natives are Rough Rider Hall of Fame member Casper Oimoen, winner of more than 20 medals and 400 trophies in skiing tournaments in Norway and later America, as well as the gallery's chief artist, Vern Skaug. U.S. Air Force four-star general David C. Jones, former chairman of the Joint Chiefs of Staff, and professional golfer Mike Morley also call the city "home." Dakota Boys Ranch outside of town offers a haven for troubled teen-agers. The North Central Experiment Station and Seed Farm is located south of the city on U.S. 83.

Immediately northwest on U.S. Highway 52 is the settlement of **Burlington** (762), built atop deposits of lignite coal. That resource and early hopes for the city inspired a heated battle with Minot for the Ward County seat; the loss of that opportunity in 1888 presaged a future of optimism followed by decline. In 1892, as construction crews of the Soo Line approached, L.M. Davis built an underground mine to serve both area settlers and steam locomotives. He also established a brickyard near the mine, using lignite to fire kilns that made bricks from local clay. But the mining business dwindled in the 1920s. In 1933 U.S. Rehabilitation Corporation stepped in to offer unemployed miners assistance by dividing a parcel of several hundred acres into lots for homes. The government's own mine was the last to operate in Burlington. Today picnics, softball games and social gatherings center around Old Settlers Park.

Des Lacs (212) made national headlines in 1922 by electing a complete ticket of women officials. **Berthold** (485) earned its name because it was point on the Great Northern nearest to the Fort Berthold Reservation some 40 miles away. Other Ward County towns include **Hartland**, **Kenaston** and **Niobe**.

Mountrail County begins in **Tagus**, named for a river in Spain; **Blaisdell** (originally Grenada) and **Palermo** (97), after the Italian city. Though Italians are scarce, many of the workers who built the railroad were of that background, along with gangs of Japanese and Greek laborers.

The area from **Ross** (104) to Stanley is the home of many Bohemians who trace their roots to a writer — a prolific correspondent for Bohemian newspapers who came in 1905 and sent word of the area's attractions far and wide. Syrians, many of them originally followers of the Islamic faith, settled the area near Ross at the turn of the century. They worshipped in a basement mosque and observed Moslem holy days such as Ramadan, when they fasted for 30 days (taking food only

(Above) The Minot Air Force Base attracts thousands of visitors during its annual open house, giving area residents a first-hand look at America's military readiness. (Below) The Norsk Host Fest is regularly listed as one of America's top 100 attactions.

after dark). A large group of Finnish people from the Iron Range of northern Minnesota settled in the nearby **Belden** area in 1903.

Stanley (1,031), the Mountrail County seat, is in the midst of a nearly level area described in 1906 by the local newspaper editor as "the most productive soil on earth, insomuch that if you stick a nail in the ground at night, it will grow into a crowbar before morning." The Lostwood National Wildlife Refuge is north on N.D. Highway 8. It may be the best surviving example of midgrass prairie pothole wetlands in all of America.

Powers Lake (466) has earned widespread attention with the National Shrine of Our Lady of the Prairies directed by the late Father Frederic Nelson. Beginning in 1953, Nelson established a parochial school system

through junior college level and home for the aged as well as the shrine itself, all in keeping with his staunch and controversial defense of older, more conservative Catholic philosophies. He was censured by the Bismarck Diocese and ultimately forbidden to administer the sacraments, an order which he defied. Nelson continued to celebrate the Tridentine Mass (used from the 16th century until Vatican II) until his death in 1988.

Sizeable walleyes have been caught on Smishek Lake, an impoundment northwest of town. Both Powers Lake Park and the Lonetree Campground to the southeast offers free camping and other facilities.

Other Burke towns include **Columbus** (325), **Larson**, **Lignite** (322), **Coteau** and **Battleview**. Columbus Larson gave his first

91

Des Lacs National Wildlife Refuge at Kenmare

name to one town and his last to the next. The source of Lignite's and Coteau's names are obvious, but Battleview's is less clear than it might seem. It stands on the site of a Mandan or Hidatsa village whose fortifications are still clearly seen on the surrounding prairie, suggesting a history of hostilities with the Sioux; no more modern engagement shows up in the history books as a source of its name.

In pioneer days **Bowbells** (587) was the site of a large ranch with its own 60-acre stockyard. Thousands of cattle were shipped eastward by rail; its loading dock could handle eight rail cars at a time. The cattle operation was closed in 1896, same year that first homesteaders arrived. Northgate Dam offers camping along with fishing for bluegills and crappies. The former pit of the Bowbells Lignite Mine has also been stocked with trout and perch.

Flaxton (182) hosts the Burke County Fair each July. Most of the townsite was seeded to flax at the time the city was founded in 1901. To the north are two ports of entry to Saskatchewan named for the border crossing: **Portal** (238), which is open 24 hours a day, and **Northgate** (9 a.m.-10 p.m.).

Des Lacs National Wildlife Refuge surrounds North and South Des Lacs Lakes on the Des Lacs River. It's the summer home of countless white pelicans, ducks and geese, and also sports a photo blind near the dancing grounds of the sharp-tailed grouse.

Kenmare (1,456) is best known as the seat of North Dakota's largest Danish settlement. The Danish wind-driven flour mill in the town square dates from about 1900 and was in use through the mid-1920s. Danish immigrants founded Brorson Parochial High School north of the city in 1906 to educate their own children along with older immigrants still arriving from Denmark at the time. It was closed after World War I. Those pioneers' story and that of other area settlers are the subject of the Lake County Pioneer Village and Museum, whose name requires explanation:

Kenmare is best known as North Dakota's largest Danish settlement and for its excellent waterfowl hunting. A park in the town square is the home of this wind-driven flour mill, used until 1920. Waterfowl thrive in the protection of the Des Lacs National Wildlife Refuge which also provides a scenic background for the city.

It reflects the would-be moniker of a county proposed at the time Ward was divided that would have included Renville, Burke and part of Mountrail as well as the Gooseneck section of Ward. Among its 15 buildings include a blacksmith shop, fanning mill, dress shop and others, all open daily during the summer. Kenmare was briefly the home of aviation pioneer Otto Timm, who gave Charles Lindbergh his first plane ride in Lincoln, Neb. in 1920.

Donnybrook (139) was named by Soo Line officials for the fair in Donnybrook, Ireland. The derivation of **Carpio** (244) might be Spanish for "city of tents." It could also reflect a blunt description of the first post office, a railroad car with the letters "P" and "O" painted on its side. **Foxholm** reflects the city in England. There's good fishing on nearby Lake Darling.

You can still glimpse the past of **Glenburn** (454) in the Glenburn Community Centennial Museum. Just to the west, **Grano** boasts the smallest 1980 population on the North Dakota highway map, reporting just six residents.

The Upper Souris National Wildlife Refuge on Lake Darling is one of 62 federal wildlife refuges in North Dakota totalling 290,000 acres, along with another 900,000 managed as waterfowl production areas or maintained through wetlands easements. (Only 16, including this one, are manned.) Birders flock to the area. Among unusual sightings are Sprague's pipit, the eared grebe, and Baird's and LeConte's sparrows.

An early church in the county seat of **Mohall** (1,049) serves as the Renville County Historical Museum. The group has also moved the restored Soo Line depot to its site.

Memorial Day is the big event of the year at **Sherwood** (294), which since 1937 has hosted (along with Estevan, Sask.) a joint U.S.-Canadian ceremony honoring fallen warriors. Flags are exchanged by honor guards to the tune of Saskatchewan bagpipes and several

Each Memorial Day in Sherwood includes a contingent of Canadian veterans for a special ceremony on the international border.

marching bands at the border station three miles north of town. Canadian and U.S. dignitaries take part in a ceremony afterwards in the school gym, followed by a community picnic, softball games and a street dance.

Mouse River Park four miles north of **Tolley** (103) offers a bit of picturesque relaxation in the Souris bottoms, with good prospects for hooking pike, walleye, perch, bullheads and smallmouth bass from the river bank or boats. Other Renville County towns include **Loraine** (21), **Norma** and **Tolley** (103).

Lansford (294) hosts Threshermen's Days on the second weekend of July. Sponsored by the Lansford Threshers and Historical Society, it harks back to the not-so-distant times before the combine. The local Pioneer Village — with the original depot, VanBuren school, a church from Grano and an 1883 log house — is open during summer.

Antler (101) earned brief fame during the early 1980s when a local farmer pledged to give free lots to families who'd emigrate to Antler and raise children; his goal was to keep the local school open. Tiny Tim gave a benefit concert on the project's behalf, and several families did take him up on his offer. Today a retired entrepreneur, Ross Kiliper, has purchased and restored some of its original buildings intending to make Antler "Christmas Town USA." In several children's books he recounts the story of the city's hospitality to Santa Claus on an emergency stop on Christmas Eve of 1906 and how it earned the saintly elf's lasting affection.

The name of **Westhope** (741) reflected early settlers' optimism for the area's agricultural future. The local branch of the county historical society has restored an early doctor's office as an arts center and museum. A number of other Soo Line towns in the area include **Landa** (62), **Roth**, **Souris** (122) and **Carbury**.

The J. Clark Salyer II National Wildlife Refuge here is the largest of the developed refuges in North Dakota, encompassing 59 miles of Souris River bottomlands from **Bantry** to the Canadian border. Explore its marshes, wooded river bottoms and sand hills on the 22-mile auto tour which begins north of **Upham** (227). The refuge provides a tree nursery, marshland wildlife observation blinds, observation towers and picnic areas. It is one of the few nesting habitats for LeConte's sparrow in the midwest. After giant Canada goose had been exterminated as a breeding bird before 1930, the U.S. Fish and Wildlife Service began a reintroduction here in 1938, followed by restocking at Upper Souris, Lostwood, Audubon and Slade refuges. Thirteen miles of the winding Souris within the refuge populated by beaver, wood ducks, white-tailed deer, muskrats and raccoons are included in the National Canoe Trail System.

While agriculture remains the region's staple industry, tourism ranks high in

Bottineau (2,829) and the surrounding Turtle Mountains. Bottineau County is also the easternmost of North Dakota's five top oil-producing counties. Both are named for Pierre Bottineau, the prominent Pembina area leader, guide and Minnesota territorial legislator who's thought to have been the first white child born in North Dakota.

This area takes its turtles seriously. A 60-foot green-and-yellow figure of Tommy the Turtle riding on a snowmobile presides over the city park on the east edge of town. The new Bottineau County Historical Museum includes an 1887 school and displays on local history. (Neighboring Boissevain, Man. — host of the Canadian Turtle Derby each August — has its own enormous terrapin as well as the Moncur Gallery of prehistoric artifacts and the Beckoning Hills Museum.) Special events include the Bottineau County Fair in June, and the Lake Metigoshe Triathlon and the

The Turtle Mountains are a year-around playground, offering outdoors activities like hiking, boating, fishing and in winter, downhill and cross-country skiing on wooded trails.

Lake Metigoshe is one of North Dakota's rare four seasons resorts...combining the best of summer and winter with comfortable accommodations. The favorable climate of the Turtle Mountains allows for a variety of outdoors activities the whole family can enjoy.

County Rodeo, both in August. Amateur theatre productions are scheduled each year at the Sawmill Playhouse north of the city.

Bottineau, the county seat, is the home of a branch of North Dakota State University, a two-year junior college that includes the Institute of Forestry and Turtle Mountain School of Para-Medical Technique. The campus has been serving students since 1907.

Lake Metigoshe State Park 14 miles northeast of Bottineau — established in 1937 and initially improved by the Works Progress Administration — is one of North Dakota's most popular vacation spots. It encompasses both Hemeric Point and Butte St. Paul, with its stunning long-distance view. Facilities including modern and primitive campgrounds, a boat ramp, picnic areas, and an outdoor amphitheatre for programs by the park naturalist Thursday through Sunday. The woods are teeming with wildlife, from deer, elk and moose to porcupines, woodchucks, beavers, mink, muskrats...and of course turtles. Spring and autumn guarantee good bird-watching as hundreds of thousands of migratory waterfowl pass through the area.

Take a dip in the cool green water along the swimming beach. Sample the rolling hills, aspen forests and small lakes echoing with the cries of loons along the Old Oak Trail, an official National Recreational Trail with boardwalks, nature blinds and overlook towers. Winter sports are outstanding, with snowmobiling and three excellent Nordic ski trails overlooking scenic vistas adding up to a total of 125-plus miles of groomed trails among the Turtle Mountains.

Private cabins ring the rest of the lake, largest of the dozens tucked between the hills. Turtle Mountain Lodge offers year-round accommodations (including boat rentals in summer) along with dining, conference facilities and an indoor pool. Resorts include Four Seasons and Crookstons'. Club de Skinautique, an exhibition water-skiing group of 40 teens, performs on the lake on

Independence Day and again in August; they appear throughout the region during the rest of the summer.

Cross Roads Range (directly east of the park on the road to St. John) is a family-oriented Christian campground and retreat center best known for its unique Conestoga Campouts recreating a pioneer wagon train traversing woods and prairies. Trail rides, hayrides and special weekend events are also on the agenda. Camp Metigoshe, established in the mid-1930s, welcomes Lutheran youth to week-long Bible sessions on Pelican Lake. The public is invited to special events such as the June folk festival and the annual auction of 80 original quilts in July. Sunday worship takes place at Lakeside Chapel on Lake Metigoshe.

Bottineau Winter Park employs the area's slopes in the interest of snow-crazed recreation. It boasts a total of eight downhill slopes, T-bar lifts and snow-making machinery along with ski rental and a snack bar in its picturesque toasty warm chalet. The park's longest run is 1,500 feet with 250-foot vertical drop.

Two state forests are located here in North Dakota's largest natural tract of woodlands. Homen State Forest is six miles east of Lake Metigoshe, home to more than 100 species of nesting birds. Turtle Mountain State Forest five miles west of Metigoshe along Strawberry Lake is the state's largest, with 5,010 acres; its dominant species are oak and aspen, with pockets of paper birch, green ash, American elm, balsam poplar and willow. Some 45 miles of scenic horseback and hiking trails wind through the heavy woods here and in the Twisted Oaks, Dahlen, Pelican Lake and Hartley Boundary areas.

In North Dakota as in the rest of the world, most monuments and memorials honor those who have been involved in wars as soldiers, leaders or victims. That makes the **International Peace Garden** even more unique, for here the people of North Dakota

The Peace Tower straddles the international border between the United States and Canada, offering a stunning backdrop to the floral beauty of the gardens.

The International Peace Garden marks the midpoint of the longest peaceful border in the world with natural forests, jewel-like lakes and a large garden of colorful flowers and plants in the beautiful setting of the Turtle Mountains. A fountain and moat mark the exact border line between the United States and Canada.

and Manitoba have built a beautiful park dedicated to peace. The 2,339-acre Peace Garden area includes not only dazzling formal plantings of foliage and flowers (more than 80,000 annuals each summer plus perennial varieties). Three auto tours and many hiking trails lead through verdant Turtle Mountain forests and past pristine Lakes Udall and Stormon.

Several buildings accommodate group events on both sides of the international border. Campgrounds for tenters and RVs are set among the trees. The central plaza features a 12-foot clock with a face of flowers, a sunken garden and reflecting pool, the Peace Tower, a carillon that chimes on the quarter hour, and the Peace Chapel — a spot for meditation on quotes from those who loved peace from Gandhi to Kennedy.

The idea of a horticultural memorial to peace was conceived by Dr. Henry Moore of Islington, Ontario, in 1929 to the Professional Grounds Management Society. The group chose this site on the longest north-south road in the world, U.S. Highway 281 (and Manitoba 10), and about midway between the Atlantic and Pacific coasts. On July 14, 1932, 50,000 people gathered to dedicate the cairn that stands straddles the precise spot of the border just inside the main entrance. It's inscribed "To God in his glory...we two nations dedicate this garden and pledge ourselves that as long as man shall live we will not take up arms against one another." The Civilian Conservation Corps built the first building, a lodge, during that decade, using rock from North Dakota and logs from Manitoba's Riding Mountain National Park. The tablets of the Ten Commandments which stand beside the lodge was dedicated in 1956 by Charlton Heston, who played Moses in the film "The Ten Commandments."

Civic, professional and fraternal groups from the American state and the Canadian province have contributed millions of dollars toward the development of the garden, which is operated as a non-profit organization managed by a board of ten directors from each nation. Among their contributions are the Carillon Bell Tower, the work of North Dakota veterans groups; the Peace Chapel, funded by the General Grand Chapter Order of Eastern Star; Masonic Auditorium, funded by Manitoba and North Dakota lodges and built in the shape of their emblem, and a variety of improvements funded by the North Dakota and National Homemakers Councils and the Manitoba Women's Institute.

The peace garden hosts thousands of talented young people each summer for the programs of the International Music Camp as well as the Royal Canadian Legion Athletic Camp. The music camp (which includes drama and visual art as well) employs about 100 artist-teachers each summer to instruct more than 2,000 junior and senior high school students and adults in the fine arts. They perform for parents and visitors in the outdoor amphitheatre at the end of each week-long session. The music camp and Peace Garden co-host several major regional events each summer including the Old-Time Fiddlers Contest in June and the International Festival of the Arts in July.

The town of **Maxbass** (141) was named for Max Bass, the famous Great Northern Railroad immigration agent. His greatest achievement was the recruitment of many German Baptist Brethren (also called Dunkards) to northwestern North Dakota, often at the church's annual conferences in Muncie, Ind. His influence is also felt in other Soo towns like **Eckman**, **Russell** (18), **Kramer** (84), **Gardena** (66) and **Overly** (25). The oddly named **Omemee** (18) is based on the Chippewa word for pigeon or turtledove.

Sund's Heavenly Fudge has put **Newburg** (151) on the chocolate lovers' map. Primarily a Christmas treat, it comes in several flavors including penuche (brown-sugar fudge), angel pecan and good old-fashioned chocolate. Larson's Museum, a private collection of farm

Young people from throughout the world come to the Peace Garden each summer to attend the International Music Camp. Weekend concerts, ranging from classical to jazz, and drama and dance, are popular with visitors.

machinery and household antiques, is located just north of town and open by appointment.

Members of St. Paul Lutheran Church of **Willow City** (329) print and assemble braille editions of St. Matthew's gospel for distribution to the blind.

Angling south on U.S. 281, travelers enter Rolette County, named for territorial leader Joseph Rolette who in 1870 became North Dakota's first homesteader. That was no small achievement, since the nearest land office was in Vermilion, S.D.

Dunseith (625) is distinguished by the W'eel Turtle, a giant turtle 40 feet long, 28 feet wide and 15 feet high built entirely of discarded car wheels. McKay's Pioneer Log Cabin Museum several miles south on N.D. Highway 5 features original furnishings in an authentically renovated log cabin from the early 1900s. The campus of San Haven north of the city is currently unused; built as a tuberculosis sanitarium in the 1930s, it most recently was operated as a branch of the Grafton State School caring for its most severely multi-handicapped residents.

Belcourt (1,900) is the center of government on the Turtle Mountain Indian Reservation. Visitors can sample its history and the culture of the Chippewa people at the Belcourt Heritage Center, which features a native American art gallery, dioramas and a gift shop. Ceremonial dances are scheduled throughout the summer. But some visitors may feel they already know the reservation through Louise Erdrich's award-winning novels *Love Medicine* and *The Beet Queen*, both set in part in this area.

Rolla (1,538), the Rolette County seat, is on the eastern edge of the rolling Turtle Mountains. Among local homesteaders at its founding in 1888 were Harry Downing, a former page boy and butler to English royalty, and his wife Marie Downing Williams, a woman who left a post as lady in waiting to Queen Victoria. Mrs. Williams later ran a Rolla rooming house, whose denizens ate from solid silver given her by the queen. The town was briefly the site of Rolla University, which was established in 1889 with 45 students but closed soonafter. John Burke, three-term governor, U.S. Treasurer and chief justice of the U.S. Supreme Court, lived here during 15 years of his youth. The William Langer Jewel Bearing Plant and a more recent facility which manufactures dosimeters employ area residents, many of them Indian residents of the Turtle Mountain Reservation. Rolla's curling team won the 1984 Junior World Curling Championship. (Another North Dakota team from Grand Forks won in 1979.)

St. John (401) was established by early missionary John Malo. It's the state's second oldest town; settlers arrived along the old Wakopa Trail in the 1840s. Nature trails follow that venerable route in Wakopa Game

Management Area eight miles west of town and at the Game and Fish Field Station and wildlife management areas. A small herd of bison are maintained by the local Izaak Walton League at Buffalo Park east of the city. At Lake Upsilon, the league has preserved a log cabin built in the 1920s of logs cut by man and beaver, each corner constructed in a different style.

The Rolette County Historical Society has brought together an early church, one-room school and log cabin, along with early railroad cars and displays related to early Indian and white history. It's open on summer Sundays.

Also of local interest are St. John the Baptist Church, built of local fieldstone; St. Claude Historic Park, site of the region's first settlement, also begun by Father Malo; and Coghlan Castle, an elaborate but now abandoned house along Highway 30 built in the Richardson Romanesque style.

The area's lakes offer varied opportunities for anglers. Gravel Lake is one of the state's best spots for whopper rainbow trout; the record tiger muskie (a 40-pounder fattened on

those trout) was caught here in 1975. Northerns, walleyes and smallmouth bass are found in Dion Lake. Rainbow and cutthroat trout swim the waters of Hooker Lake, and Lake Upsilon offers pike. Set among the lakes are **Nanson, Mylo** (31) and **Agate**.

The Towner County Service Memorial is at **Rock Lake** (287). Pike, perch and bluegills abound at Big Coulee Dam near **Bisbee** (257). The Towner County Historical Society sponsors several events at its museum in **Egeland** (112) including an ice cream social, art show and the North Dakota One Cylinder Stationary Engine Show in June. The museum is flanked by Larsen's Blacksmith Shop and the city's original fieldstone jail.

Cando (1,496) is the unofficial capital of North Dakota's Durum Triangle, the multi-county area where 85 percent of the nation's durum wheat ripens each summer. It's also the site of Noodles by Leonardo, a

Gravel hole is one of North Dakota's best for rainbow trout.

100

At the intersection of U.S. 2 and ND 3 is the cairn marking the geographical center of North America at Rugby. (Below) Near Verendrye is the spherical David Thompson Memorial, commemorating the British geographer who explored the center of the continent on the eve of the 19th century.

manufacturing plant which turns durum into semolina and semolina in turn to high-quality pasta. Its products are sold under its own premium label as well as house labels for various firms. The Towner County Fair takes place each June. The renovated First State Bank building now houses the Cando Pioneer Foundation's displays and the local senior citizens' center. Cando is the home of Vikings football player Dave Osborne.

West on U.S. Highway 2 is **Leeds** (678), named for an English town. Like so many towns, its founders had hopes of the highest order. A boomer newspaper editor wrote, "A man died and entered heaven. On his first walk about his new abode he noticed several men fettered in ball and chain. His inquiry of a passer-by brought the reply, 'They came from Leeds, North Dakota, and if they weren't chained they'd go back.'"

Lake Ibsen southeast of Leeds, named for the Norwegian playwright Henrik Ibsen, was prominent in recent Indian history as the spot where the Sioux and Chippewa made a peace treaty in 1858. Early visitors knew the area to the east as Petites Isles Aux Mortes, or "small islands of the dead." Area Indians carried the bodies of many victims of smallpox to small islands in Lake Aux Mortes to be laid on scaffolds, visible for miles along the shore.

The Ralph and Evangeline Pierson farmhouse south of **York** (69) was the first in North Dakota to become electrified through the Rural Electrification Program, a distinction commemorated by inclusion in the National Register of Historic Places. Power surged through the lines on Thanksgiving Eve, 1937. Wiring had been ready to go since 1923 as part of the structure of the house, which like many of its day was purchased from a mail order catalog. York's neighbor **Knox** (69) is named in honor of John Knox, the Scottish religious reformer.

Chippewa Indians performed tribal dances in **Pleasant Lake** until territorial times. The shallow body of water which shares that name

was called Broken Bones Lake by Indians who camped along its shores during buffalo hunts; they broke the bison bones to remove marrow, which they preserved for winter use.

Other Benson County towns along the Soo Line include **Billmore**, **Baker**, **Harlow**, **Brinsmade** (54), **Esmond** (337), **Flora** and **Oberon** (150).

Maddock (677), south on N.D. 30, is the home of Summers Manufacturing, which builds farm implements especially suited to conditions in the northern plains including the Herman culti-harrow and diamond disk.

Rugby (3,355) is the center of more than Pierce County government. Here a tapering 18-foot monument of fieldstone marks the approximate center of the North American continent, a point on which the city has capitalized since the U.S. Geological Survey located the spot in 1932. The monument — built by local Boy Scouts — stands atop a heart-shaped base on land provided by owners of a Texaco station, a point that caused some consternation in 1970. When the service station owners moved their business across the road that year, they took their monument with them. Surprised travelers were told the continent had eroded a bit and the monument had to be moved to correct the matter. The gas station is only one of a plethora of Rugby enterprises that capitalize on the same fact, including the Center Motel, The Hub truck stop, the Cornerstone Cafe and the Heart of America library.

How does Rugby know it's at the heart of things? The Geological Survey determined the continent's center by constructing a large model from firm fabric, then placing it in a vacuum and balancing it on an ultra-fine point which happened to coincide with Rugby (or at least Pierce County). The designation was tirelessly promoted during the '30s by local members of the Canal to Canada Highway Association of towns along U.S. Highway 3. Since those days the Geological Survey has pinned the center down a bit more precisely, locating it in a pothole six miles west of Balta (south of Rugby). That's of little importance to the Geographical Center Pioneer Village and Museum which borders that old familiar stone cairn. Among its displays are antique cars and farm machinery and extensive local memorabilia related to the area's Scandinavian and German-Russian heritage. The village includes a jail, consolidated school and church.

Rugby's Pierce County Courthouse, built in 1910, is on the National Register of Historic Places. It features original scenes of everyday life in the city's early days inside its dome. One of Rugby's more famous natives was florist N.P. Lindberg, who coined the slogan "Say It With Flowers." Today Rugby Manufacturing builds truck box bodies and hoists for worldwide distribution. The city hosts the State Championship Horse Show in June, featuring several parades among a full schedule of equestrian events.

The Dakota Hawk Foundation Museum northeast of **Wolford** includes an extensive display of fully restored antique tractors and implements, plus much more farming and household equipment. Among them are a one-of-a-kind 1912 Hackney Auto Plow, a dog-powered treadmill, a 1934 Plymouth coupe, a 1912 Metz Gray tractor. Created the late Dale Hawk and his wife Martha, a non-profit foundation now operates thee museum, which is open afternoons seven days a week. Other towns: **Barton** (38), **Silva**, **Selz**.

Balta Dam south of **Balta** (139) offers fishing, swimming and camping. The shrine of Mary the Center of America — built entirely of native stone — stands on the Wendelin Bickler farm near **Orrin**, where its creator also maintains a rock museum of every conceivable variety including lunar samples.

Towner (867), the McHenry County seat, has long called itself the "Cattle Capital of North Dakota." It's named for Col. O.M. Towner, an early-day bonanza rancher. It does well with horses, too; the state's largest quarter horse ranch is located nearby, and Tuesday night races are a local tradition. Towner hosts a major rodeo on Independence Day, and the county historical society holds a flea market each fall on the grounds of its museum, the former Zion Lutheran Church. The products of local dairy cows and bees are processed here at Winger Cheese and Gunter Honey. The Towner Nursery two miles north of town is operated by the North Dakota Forest Service, which produces more than 1.2 million spruce, pine and juniper seedlings each year for planting through the Soil Conservation Service.

During the 1880s the Towner area attracted a large number of wealthy Englishmen including several members of the nobility, perhaps through James J. Hill's promotion of the fertile land and his backing by British financial interests. At least some of these atypical settlers were "remittance men," younger sons of aristocratic households paid a good-sized annual allowance to keep out of England and avoid embarrassing their families. Among their number were Joseph and Brian Barclay (reputed to be English lords), their relative Pieraeut, Edmund Thursby (who imported purebred Angus cattle from Scotland), Coutts Marjoribanks (younger son of the Baron of Tweedmouth) and his sister Lady Ishbel, Marchioness of Aberdeen, prominent in England's suffrage movement. Her husband later became the governor general of Canada. Scandinavian immigrant Sondre Norheim, the world's first champion ski jumper, is buried in the yard of Norway Lutheran Church.

N.D. Highway 14 continues through **Bantry** (28), **Upham** (227) and **Denbigh**. Many residents of **Granville** (281), named for Great Northern engineer Granville Dodge, were once scolded by a local editor who deplored the number of "old bachelors who do not improve their places and so many old maids holding down claims. It ought to cause a blush of

Amid the potholes and pastures, the hardy state flower, the Wild Prairie Rose, blooms all summer long.

102

shame to mount the face of every bald-headed old bachelor in the vicinity." Not unexpectedly, fishing and hunting are popular pastimes on nearby Buffalo Lodge Lake, which also has camping facilities.

The Denbigh Experimental Forest here was established on a full section of land in 1931 to determine which trees and bushes could survive on the northern Great Plains. The Skyline Trail curls through stands of ponderosa pine, sand dunes and rugged landscape. Birdwatchers watch out for pine warblers and black-backed three-toed woodpeckers.

Several German Mennonite settlements surround **Surrey** (999) — some from earlier settlements in Pennsylvania, and others from the German colonies of Russia's Black Sea.

The alternate route beginning at Churchs Ferry continues south on U.S. 281 past **Minnewaukan** (461). The city stood at the western end of Devils Lake in settlement days; steamboats landed at what is now the Benson County Fairgrounds.

For more than 40 years **New Rockford** (1,761) has been the site of a major Steam Thresher Show in September. Steam and gas engines for threshing, sawing lumber, making shingles. Daily parades of steam engines and antique cars; exhibits of quilts, demonstrations of lefse, fiddlers jamboree.

The Ralph Hall farm ten miles south of New Rockford has been recognized for its stately neoclassical architectural style by inclusion in the National Register of Historic Places. It was built by Ralph Hall, a state legislator, county sheriff and federal agent to the Fort Totten Indian Reservation. His grandson Ralph Harmon now farms the property. Besides the house (built in 1910), the farmstead includes a huge barn dating from 1898 and 1926 garage.

The Burlington Northern line crosses into Wells County here, passing **Hamberg** (41), **Wellsburg, Heimdal** and **Bremen**.

Fessenden (761), the county seat, faces U.S. Highway 52. Its Queen Anne Revival-style courthouse, built in 1895 by architect J.W. Ross, has been renovated by county commissioners in recent years. The county historical museum is located on the Wells County Fairgrounds in the two-room Emrick School. The 1988 county fair here introduced the first parimutuel betting permitted under a new North Dakota law, adding cash stakes to Fessenden's long tradition of horse racing. A number of horse farms in the vicinity raise and train racing stock.

A glimpse of the city in the 1920s appears in Richard Critchfield's acclaimed family history entitle *Those Days: An American Album*. Critchfield, son of a country doctor whose family lived there for seven years, became a noted foreign correspondent, author and scholar. Other reminders of those days (and others as well) are on display at the Wells County Museum.

Harvey (2,527) hosts the North Dakota Softball Hall of Fame at Veterans Memorial Field; it's open during softball tournaments and by appointment. Like its neighbor **Martin** (114), Harvey is surrounded by a sportsmen's paradise, with solid fishing at Harvey Dam and hunting the pothole country for grouse, duck, goose and deer. Several guide services stand ready to help locate moving targets. Butte de Morale, which rises 300 feet above the prairie, was a locus of Metis buffalo hunting parties of the 1840s; one party of 1,400 people in 824 wagons camped here, slaughtering 250 bison on a single day.

The name of **Anamoose** (355) comes from "uhnemoosh," the Chippewa word for dog. Other area towns include **Drake** (479), **Balfour** (51), **Kief** (36), **Butte** (157), **Ruso** (12) and **Karlsruhe** (164). Many Ukrainian families live in the vicinity, the descendants of Protestant immigrants who came seeking religious freedom from the Russian Orthodox Church. Dogden Butte, from which the **town** of Butte draws its name, was a landmark on

the mail route from Fort Totten to **Fort Stevenson**; located within territory controlled by the Sioux, its sighting opened up the everpresent possibility of ambush. The Garrison Diversion Conservancy District operates its North Central Irrigation Experiment Station near Karlsruhe.

One of North Dakota's least visited historic sites is near **Verendrye**. A handsome sphere of granite honors geographer David Thompson, who passed the spot in 1797 on a scientific expedition southward from British Canada to explore the Upper Missouri country. **Bergen** (24) and **Voltaire** (65) are youngsters in the midst of towns dating from the late 1800s, both incorporated in 1929. **Sawyer** (417) is much older, welcoming its first homesteader in 1882.

Basin Electric's William J. Neal Station generates electricity from North Dakota's easternmost deposit of lignite. It's near the town of **Velva** (1,101), home of internationally famous broadcaster Eric Sevareid. In his autobiography *Not So Wild a Dream* he reflected on the nation's emerging social consciousness in the 1930s, "It occurred to me then that what men wanted was Velva, on a national, on a world, scale."

More than 30 years after leaving the state, Sevareid observed, "There is a curious bond between people who have lived in North Dakota and meet one another in other places around the country and the world... The words 'North Dakota' have always called up memories, not just of a place, but of a special kind of life, bleak and yet rich, full of hardships and of longings for something over the horizon, an existence that was a matter of mutual dependency, yet one of freedom, of space and infinitude. I suppose one should feel no pride over his place of origin; he couldn't help where he was born. But we're all human and I must admit that I am very, very satisfied with my own origins. I wouldn't trade my boyhood for that of any other man." III

103

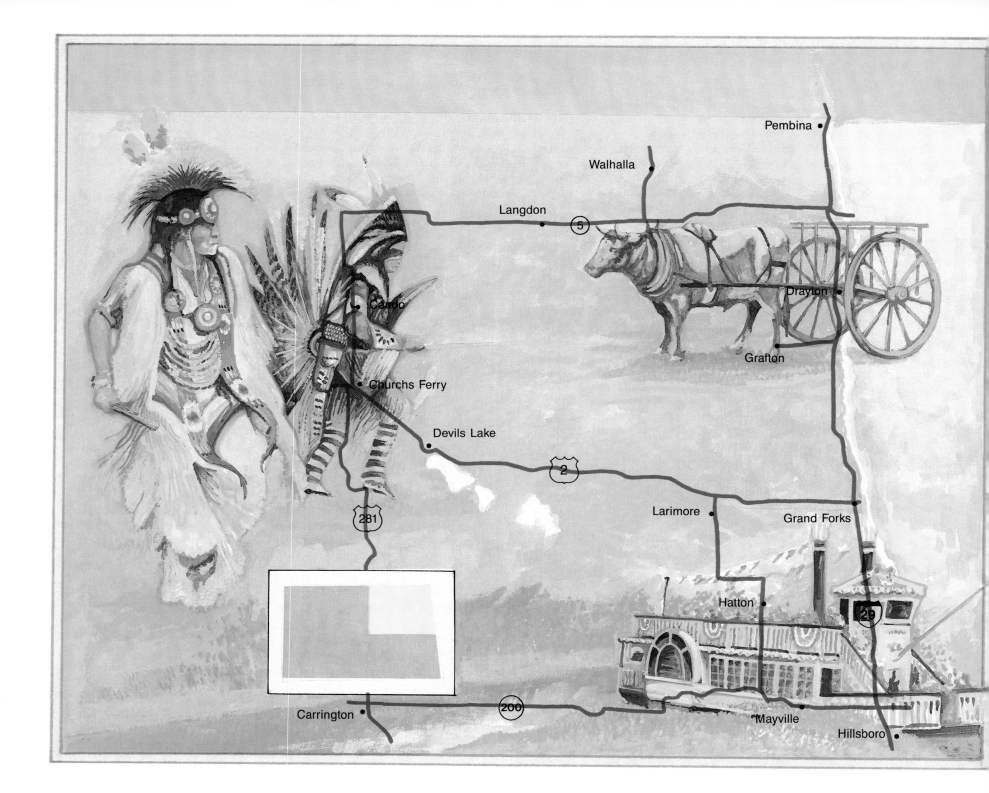

Pembina

Walhalla

Langdon

⑤

Drayton

Cando

Grafton

Churchs Ferry

Devils Lake

②

Larimore

Grand Forks

281

Hatton

29

Carrington

200

Mayville

Hillsboro

Roots and the Red River

The highlights: White settlement in North Dakota began here, in the northeastern quarter of the state in the fertile lake bed of ancient Lake Agassiz. French and English fur traders opened the upper Red River Valley on the eve of the nineteenth century. They were followed across the years by ox cart drovers and blue-clad soldiers, wheat farmers and railroad barons, and the settlements that sprang up in their tracks.

The route: Starting at Grand Forks, head west on U.S. Highway 2 to Devils Lake and Fort Totten. Turn south at Churchs Ferry on U.S. 281 to eastbound N.D. Highway 200 past Finley and Mayville (with a detour to Hatton and Northwood) to Interstate 29. After a stop in Hillsboro, return north to Grand Forks. Or choose an alternate route: North on I-29 past Grafton to Pembina, then west on N.D. 5 past Langdon to its intersection with U.S. 281 at Rock Lake; south on 281 to Cando and beyond, then back via U.S. 2.

Welcome to **Grand Forks** (43,7765). Called Les Grandes Fourches by French Canadian explorers and traders who probed the area in the late 1700s, it owes its early importance to its strategic site at the junction of Red and Red Lake Rivers. Permanent settlement began here in 1868 with a way station on the mail route from Fort Pembina to Fort Abercrombie, making this the oldest of North Dakota's major cities.

Like most of northeastern North Dakota's historical roots, the seeds of settlement were sown not by the United States to the south and east, but by British and French interests in Canada. The furious and often vicious competition of the XY Company, North West Fur Company and Hudson's Bay Company set the stage for reaping the first economic benefit from the upper Red River Valley.

The Earl of Selkirk's idealistic scheme to relocate the poor of Scotland and Ireland in the wilderness of the Canadian northwest brought the first farmers south of what would become the international line. Members of the Selkirk colony raised their first crops at Pembina and hunted Dakota buffalo in the summer of 1812.

Canada-based explorers knew this country well before Lewis and Clark's epic expedition of discovery opened the Upper Missouri. Pierre Gaultier de Varennes, Sieur de la Verendrye, scrutinized the Pembina Mountains on his 1738 journey in search of a shortcut to India, claiming the lands along his route for France in the name of King Louis XV and gaining exclusive right to the furs they would produce. In 1797 the North West Company, one of the great English fur-trading outfits, hired geographer David Thompson (who later would help fix the international boundary under the Treaty of 1818) to document an area including much of North Dakota. Its representative Charles Chaboillez chose the same date to establish the first trading post on its behalf in Pembina. Three years later partner Alexander Henry establish a trading depot in the area of Grand Forks.

Until the years after the Civil War, the land around Grand Forks was the exclusive province of Indians, traders and the colorful Metis, a distinct culture mixing the ethnic traditions of European traders and the Indians of the mid-continent. Primarily French and Chippewa, they dominated the first half of the nineteenth century not only here but north to Winnipeg and well beyond, scoffing at the border by trading freely across it and hunting buffalo here on gargantuan annual epics of slaughter.

During the first half of the 1800s, processions of hundreds of ox-drawn carts lumbered up and down the valley between Fort Garry north of Winnipeg and St. Paul, the region's two major centers. Two enormous wheels, each six feet in diameter, propelled each load of furs southward and supplies returning to the north. (Their tracks can still be seen in the city's Lincoln Park.) Two sounds defined Grand Forks in those earliest days — the squealing of those wooden wheels on wooden axles announcing the approach of Red River carts, and the songs and shouts of flatboat pilots as they propelled their heavily loaded craft north with the river's current. A rough frontier community thrived along with the trade; in 1875 it was incorporated as a city of Dakota Territory.

Two other toots would eventually be heard — the whistles of steamboats plying the curling, looping course of the Red River beginning in 1868, and the trill of steam locomotives speeding along the new Great Northern Railway in 1879. Today both remain prominent on visits to Grand Forks, though not in equal measure. Today's Burlington Northern railroad facilities (long touted as largest terminal between Minneapolis and Seattle) are best appreciated from the Columbia Road overpass just south of the University of North Dakota campus. And the faded glory of the powerful Red River can be glimpsed from the deck of the *Dakota Queen*, the comfortable modern recreation that traces several miles of winding river along voyages on the long days of summer. They recall the plaintive strains of the song "Red River Valley," written about this very place by James Kerrigan in 1896.

Modern Grand Forks is best known as the site of the University of North Dakota and a wealth of agricultural processing industries, from the State Mill and Elevator's Dakota Maid Flour to french fried potatoes for McDonald's restaurants.

The State Mill is a legacy of the socialist program of the Nonpartisan League; today as in its youth, it remains the only state-owned industry of its kind in the nation. The enterprise emerged from North Dakota farmers' dissatisfaction with the Minneapolis grain market and millers' stranglehold on their bountiful spring wheat. When the NPL gained control of the state legislature in 1919, members quickly ratified a program authorizing establishment of a number of enterprises including a state-owned system of elevators, mills, warehouses and factories. It had trouble getting off the ground even after completion in 1923 at three times its projected million-dollar cost, struggling along with

A popular summer attraction in Grand Forks is the Dakota Queen, a riverboat that carries passengers in a style reminiscent of the city's pioneer days.

operating losses until World War II. Today, with bipartisan support, the State Mill is modestly profitable. Its major product is semolina, a coarse protein-rich flour prized for high-quality pasta; this is the largest of only six producers nationwide. Its Dakota Maid Flour, with its emblem of a cheerful Indian woman, has long been sold within the region through a novel approach to advertising. For more than 50 years all state printing was required by law to carry slogan, "Buy Dakota Maid Products."

The State Mill is only one of a number of factories that produce food products from area crops. Cream of Wheat was invented in Grand Forks and manufactured here during its first

few years. Today plants owned by Pillsbury, Simplot and others turn the region's potatoes into instant mashed potato flakes, potato chips and french fries. Sugarbeets are processed at the American Crystal Sugar plant across the river in East Grand Forks. Siouxland Buffalo raises bison on a ranch near town, selling a lean red meat with a taste halfway between beef and venison with less fat, less cholesterol and fewer calories. The city is also known as the birthplace of that north country staple, the headbolt heater, though its manufacture was soon moved to Alabama.

UND, the state's largest and oldest institution of higher education, predates the

Dakotas' entry into the Union by five years. When its first classes were held in September 1884, its campus stood two miles west of the rest of the city, connected by trolley line. The university has played a larger role than the education of generations of North Dakota's young. Its faculty has conducted research on the state's geological and historical resources, a mission that continues today with archeological discoveries and the ground-breaking Energy Research Center. The buildings of the new Aerospace Center and the $7 million Northwest Aerospace Training Center testify that research begun beneath the earth will be carried on in the skies.

Medicine, law and the arts have had their due, along with programs designed to educate teachers, journalists and businesspeople. Chester Fritz Auditorium hosts national and international stars in a variety of fields, from opera and touring drama companies to country and rock music. The North Dakota Museum of Art located in West Gym has become a widely respected center, with exhibitions ranging from contemporary paintings and ceramics to fine quilts, crafts and sculpture. North Dakota sculptor Albert Reddig's red and yellow "Once Over Machine" — created of parts from a self-propelled combine — is both landmark and symbol of the museum's fresh approach to defining "art."

The campus area abounds with some of the city's most graceful homes including the houses of Fraternity Row and Oxford House, the restored presidential residence that now houses the Alumni Association. Other stately residences line Belmont Road and Reeves Avenue south of a memorial to the young city's Civil War veterans. The figure of Justice presides over the dome of the Grand Forks County Courthouse, whose interior walls are decorated with original murals and its rotunda with four painted scenes of North Dakota life.

The Grand Forks County Historical Society preserves a faithful modern replica of an early frontier home, Campbell House, as a tribute to pioneer women. It stands on the well-tended grounds of the fascinating Myra Museum along with a log post office and other early Grand Forks structures. Central Park stands on what's believed to be the site of Grand Forks' first buildings, displaying the millstone from the local flour mill which in 1877 became the first along the Red River.

West of Grand Forks near **Emerado** (596) — home of business financier John Hancock — is the Grand Forks Air Force Base, a key link in the nation's northern defense system. Now more than 30 years old, the base is the home of some 8,000 enlisted personnel and their families. It was the second in the United States to get the new B-1 bomber. The base hosts tens of thousands of civilians on the last weekend of June with Friends and Neighbors Day. Referring to its facilities and bases here and in Minot, the Air Force has said there is "more power in this area than any other single part of the planet." During the 1970s, when the nation's anti-ballistic missile network was added to northeastern North Dakota's arsenal, observers were fond of pointing out that if the state had seceded from the Union in 1933, when a state senate resolution actually called for its departure, this would be the third biggest nuclear power in the world.

Turtle River State Park surrounds the banks of a meandering little river which once tumbled vigorously along its channel, carving out a shady wooded gorge that dips below the surrounding prairie. Within the park — located 22 miles west of Grand Forks — archeologists have identified mounds built by prehistoric Indians, along with their copper

The State Mill is a "one of a kind" which today has a world-wide reputation for producing high quality semolina for pasta manufacturers.

107

by Dick Larson, UND Office of University Relations.

(Left) The Chester Fritz Auditorium near the English Coulee on the UND campus hosts a variety of concerts and performances each year. (Top) The largest and oldest university in the state, UND today is earning a reputation for aviation and aerospace studies. This helicoper flying over campus is one of several training aircraft donated by manufacturers. (Above) The gracious Stone Alumni Center, a popular tourist attraction and home of the first UND president.

instruments and ivory pipes. Begun by the Civilian Conservation Corps in the 1930s, park facilities now include a swimming pool, picnic shelters, modern and semi-modern campsites, rustic cabins and a lodge. Snowmobile and cross-country ski trails, a hill for sledding and an ice-skating rink are popular during winter, when a heated chalet offers refreshments and a chance to thaw chilly toes.

Arvilla was named for the wife of bonanza farmer H.T. Hersey, proprietor of the 2,480-acre Crystal Springs Stock Farm The Minnesota millionaire often entertained his friend James J. Hill in style, served by full staff of attentive servants. Presbyterian minister John A. Brown established the Arvilla Academy & North Dakota Conservatory of Music here in 1886 with his daughter, a graduate of the Boston Conservatory of Music, heading its music department. It burned down in 1893 and was never rebuilt.

The town of **Niagara** (76) was originally built on skids, the better to move a mile west to the side of the Great Northern upon its long-awaited arrival. The Niagara Community Historical Society maintains several historic buildings here including a log cabin from the Turtle River, a rural schoolhouse and the town's first church.

Petersburg (230) was named for a local Norwegian clergyman and **Michigan** (502) for the home state of many of its original settlers. Manville Johnson, founder of the region chain of Johnson Home Town Stores, learned the dry goods business at Michigan Mercantile in 1907, eventually going on to operate 14 small-town Johnson Stores in north and eastern North Dakota.

Mapes bears the name of Emery Mapes, one of inventors of Cream of Wheat. The

The Campbell House and Myra Museum takes visitors to Grand Forks back to pioneer days, with a special tribute to pioneer women.

nearby ghost town of **Bartlett**, once the end of the rail line, boasted 21 saloons in 1883, one featuring a black piano player who ended his nightly performances with the refrain, "Bartlett, dear Bartlett, will be a dandy of Dakota yet."

McVille Dam just east of **McVille** (626) offers good fishing for rainbow trout. The town's name is a tribute to postmaster McDougal and storekeeper McCracken. Other Nelson County towns include **Whitman**, **Dahlen**, **Pekin** (101), **Tolna** (241) and **Kloten**. **Aneta** (341) hosts a turkey barbecue each summer, roasting the locally-raised birds in a 100-foot charcoal pit.

The handsome fieldstone Episcopal church in **Lakota** (963) bears witness to the Anglo-American and Yankee families who developed many a North Dakota townsite — and then left for greener pastures, ceding their local dominance to northern European immigrant farmers. Lakota's name is the Teton Sioux variation on Dakota, the Santee Sioux word meaning allies or friends. The town's Tofthagen Library & Museum were donated in 1927 by a pioneer settler.

Past **Crary** (139) and **Doyon**, named for a bonanza farmer is one of North Dakota's most scenic areas. **Devils Lake** (7,442) was once in fact on the shore of the body of water that shares its name; between settlement in 1882 and the late 1960s, the lake receded more than five miles. Freshening its sinking waters was once of the goals of the incomplete Garrison Diversion project. Yet the lake set off on its own rehabilitation, with the current cycle of freshening and growth again changing its shoreline.

One of the first citizens of Creel City, Devils Lake's antecedent, was Edward Heerman, captain of the steamboat *Minnie H*, which plied the waters between that town at Fort Totten on the southern shore. At the turn of the century the *Minnie H* and two smaller steamers carried revelers across the waters to the Chautauqua at Lakeside Park. The entertainments at what became the nation's third largest of its kind continued until the mid-1920s, long after the shrinking lake had deep-sixed steamboat transportation.

The Lake Region Heritage Center is housed in the old Devils Lake Post Office. The Ramsey County group has also restored the former sheriff's residence, a two-story red brick building from 1912 included in the National Register of Historic Place. Private investors have renovated the unique triangular Great Northern Hotel as a business center. The North Dakota School for Deaf was established here in 1890 on park-like grounds populated by ducks and geese floating along a stream. Among its graduates is Tony Award-winning actress Phyllis Frelich. Other young people attend Lake Region Junior College. The North Dakota National Guard's Camp Grafton south of the city has since 1904 been the site of summer field training. Named for World War I hero Lt. Col. Gilbert C. Grafton, the camp occupies a small part of the former Fort Totten military reserve.

The Devils Lake State Parks are the newest addition to North Dakota's public recreation areas, the key recreational development associated with the Garrison Diversion project. There are four areas from which to choose. Graham's Island State Park is 14 miles southwest of the city of Devils Lake; it's named for Scottish fur trader Duncan Graham, who operated a post here in 1814. Shelver's Grove State Recreation Area is two miles southeast of the city. The Narrows State Recreation Area is four miles directly south on East Devils Lake, with a three-lane boat ramp and parking lot for 200 vehicles suggesting its popularity with anglers. Black Tiger Bay State Recreation Area 18 miles southwest of Devils Lake has opened up another of the lake's prime fishing area. Overnight camping is accommodated in all but the last of these areas.

Widely known in historical circles as the best-preserved military fort of the Indian Wars period, Fort Totten is a popular stop for visitors to the Devils Lake area.

The public parklands are among a total of 10 campgrounds and several resorts ringing the lake. Many boat ramps offer fishermen a launching point for expeditions in search of walleye, northern pike, perch and white bass; in winter they provide access to the burgeoning shanty towns of ice-fishing houses that dot the lake. Boats may be rented at several of the private facilities.

The Fort Totten Indian Reservation is south of the lake on N.D. Highway 20. The Indian agency was established in 1867 for the Chippewa, for whose use the area was set aside until 1882; in that year the courts opened land north of the lake to white settlement. The town of **St. Michael** was established as an Indian mission in 1874 by the Grey Nuns at the invitation of the first Indian agent, Major William Forbes. The church was very active among the local people; Father Jerome Hunt published one of the few Sioux-language newspapers here during the late 1800s. The venerable Bell Isle General Store here sells groceries along with supplies for Indian beadwork, recorded Indian music and clothing. Original beaded necklaces, earrings and bolo ties are available here among proprietor Muttsey Belisle's private collection of traditional crafts. Traffic has increased dramatically since the unoccupied mission school became the site of Dacotah Bingo. Its high-stakes games attract Bingo fanatics from throughout the area, bringing them by the busload from distant cities.

Devils Lake Sioux Manufacturing, a military subcontractor manufacturing helmets and camouflage netting, is the main

Devils Lake is a popular recreation area, famous for camping, boating and fishing for walleye and perch. Sailboat races are held each summer in addition to several fishing derbys.

enterprise in **Fort Totten**. Stark dramatic outlines in concrete delineate the new Four Winds School serving youngsters from kindergarten through senior high on the town's southern edge. The annual Fort Totten Pow Wow on the last weekend of July draws dancers and singers from throughout mid-North America to share fellowship, show off their skills, celebrate traditional Indian culture and compete for substantial cash prizes.

Fort Totten State Historic Site is considered the best-preserved military post of the Indian Wars era. Its first log buildings went up in 1867 followed by handsome structures of brick baked from clay quarried at foot of nearby Sully's Hill. After their completion, the garrison discovered that the clay was seeded with limestone pebbles which absorbed rainwater—and crumbled when wet. Thus every building was sealed with white paint as much for waterproofing as for the square's tidy appearance. Fort Totten served as a military post until 1890, then was refitted as an Indian school consolidated with the Grey Nuns' mission school from St. Michael; it was operated until 1959 with the exception of five years in the 1930s, when it was pressed into service as a preventorium for Indian youth with tuberculosis. Today it accommodates the Lake Region Pioneer Daughters Museum, a taxidermy display of birds and wildlife, and the Fort Totten Little Theatre, which stages amateur musicals each July and August.

Sully's Hill National Game Preserve dates back to 1904, when President Theodore Roosevelt set it aside as a national park on the basis of its unusual ecology. It was redesignated a big game preserve 1914 and given official refuge status in 1921. The hill is inhabited today by bison, deer and elk herds, prairie dogs, countless songbirds and waterfowl including Canada, blue and snow geese — a total of 269 species. Its facilities include picnic shelters on Sweetwater Lake and several look-out points offering a 15-mile view. Cross-country skiing trails are open to public in winter. Archeologists have identified burial mounds and other signs of habitation dating back to the Middle Woodland Culture shortly after the time of Christ.

Toward the east, Devil's Heart south of **Tokio** was used as a meeting place by the Sioux; any promise made here was said to be sacred among the Indians. Now the Benson County Park on nearby Wood Lake offers fishing and camping as well as picnic facilities. The Japanese-sounding name is actually derived from the Indian words "to-ki," or gracious gift.

Other area towns include **Warwick** (for a British earl) and **Hamar** (after the town in Norway) in Benson County. In Ramsey County (named for Minnesota Governor and U.S. Senator Alexander Ramsey) are **Hampden**, **Edmore** (416), **Webster**, **Lawton** (101), **Brocket** (74), **Southam**, **Penn** and **Starkweather** (210), whose accuracy is undisputed. The Sons of Jacob Cemetery near Garske is one of two Jewish burial grounds in the state, all that remains of a Jewish settlement from the 1880s. Among the founders' direct descendants is Stewart Stern, the Hollywood screenwriter of "Rebel Without a Cause."

Back at the junction of U.S. 2 and U.S. 281, **Churchs Ferry** (139) marks the location of a ferry across Mauvaise Coulee operated during the high water of 1886 by one Irvine Church. **Minnewaukan** (461) to the south means "holy water" in the Sioux language; the English name Devils Lake is a mistranslation. The town originally stood on the western shore of Devils Lake, with steamboats berthing at the present site of the Benson County Fairgrounds.

Sheyenne (307) shares its misspelled name with the Sheyenne River, maintaining the mistake of early explorers who intended to call it "Cheyenne" after the Indian tribe. The community made a bold attempt to refurbish its dwindling downtown in a western motif

Sully's Hill National Game Preserve is the home for such big animal species as this 'bugling elk'.

by Jim Erickson, Devils Lake

more than a decade ago. The Farmers & Merchants Bank still stands by U.S. 281 with a famous credo emblazoned on its side in peeling paint: "Nothing was ever lost through enduring faith in North Dakota." Just past New Rockford is **Barlow**, named for F.G. Barlow, a member of North Dakota's first legislature and a staunch opponent of Louisiana Lottery bill.

The Arrowwood National Wildlife Refuge 15 miles southeast of Carrington is the most fully developed in North Dakota. Its 20 miles of the James River are home to more than 250 species of birds; a bird list and auto tour brochure are available at the refuge headquarters. Local residents can help point the way to the Hawk's Nest in the same region, one of the last stands of buffalo grass and pin oaks. It offers overnight camping, hiking and (in winter) skiing and tobogganing.

Turn eastward on N.D. Highway 200 past **Glenfield** (164). Other area Foster County towns include **Grace City** (104), **Juanita**, **Bordulac** and **Melville**.

The Griggs County seat, **Cooperstown** (1,308), was established in 1880 by the Cooper brothers with profits from mining in Colorado. At the same time they founded the Sanborn, Cooperstown and Turtle Mountain Railroad and built it as far as Cooperstown. The city was the home of U.S. Senator Gerald P. Nye and Congressman James H. Sinclair. Prehistoric burial mounds have been identified east of city. The extensive collections of the Griggs County Historical Museum here boast one of the last two steam-powered popcorn machines in existence.

Lake Jessie has had its ups and downs. The alkaline waters were definitely down in 1933, when motorcycle races were held on its bone-dry bed. From 1914 through the 1920s **Binford** (293) and, indeed, all of Griggs County were famous for breeding white German shepherd dogs. Ansonia Kennels here was the largest, but a total of 400 farmers in the county were raising the puppies at the time. Also famous were the summer dances at Red Willow Lake, whose pavilion could seat 1,500 guests.

To the north, Stump Lake was originally called Lake Wamduska, the Sioux term for serpent. Legend told that an angry Great Spirit permitted a great forest here to be swallowed by water; the stumps suggest a basis for the tale. A 75-room hotel was built here in the 1880s by speculators who believed the Great Northern would pass the lakeshore; instead, the tracks were laid ten miles north. The peninsula called Bird Island has become a wildlife sanctuary.

South of Cooperstown are **Walum** and **Hannaford** (201). The latter was once a center for the sport of ski-jumping, with competitions taking place on a towering wooden structure built in defiance of the flat prairie landscape.

Steele County made headlines in the agricultural boom of the middle 1970s when the U.S. Census Bureau proclaimed that it had more millionaires per capita than any other in the United States. While that may be disputable, based as it was on land values, the area does have its share of prosperous farms.

The town of **Finley** (718) was originally one of two twin townsites; the other was Gilbert. When the Great Northern arrived in 1896, Finley's future was sealed; it grew and absorbed its twin. It was named for W.W. Finley, a former official of Jim Hill's railway who by the time of the town's establishment had resigned to become president of the Southern Railroad. Finley's largest employer, Top Taste Bakery, produces 185 varieties of frozen baked goods to serve Minnesota, Montana, North Dakota, Missouri and Iowa. Some 50,000 loaves of bread are shipped from its plant daily. Picturesque Golden Lake between Finley and Portland is a popular spot for boating, fishing, picnicking and taking life easy.

Some of the best farmland in the world is found in the Larimore-Northwood-Hatton-Mayville area of the Red River Valley.

A quick diversion north on N.D. 18 leads to **Northwood** (1,240), the center of an area famed for its endless arrow-straight shelter belts including mile after mile of fragrant lilacs. North Dakota has more acres of shelter belts than any other state, a legacy of plantings by Soil Conservation Districts in Dirty '30s. Northwood is the home of writer Pedar Nelson, an immigrant whose Norwegian-language stories of life in North Dakota were published both here and in Norway from 1918 until his death in 1979. It's also the home town of Gilmore T. Schjeldahl, inventor and adaptor of many plastics processes (including freezer bags and applications of Mylar). Schjeldahl's Twin Cities firm constructed the satellites Echo I and II and Pageos; he invented the Schjelevator, a plastic dome that stores 500,000 bushels of grain. The Northwood Pioneer Museum in old City Hall — open on summer Sundays — displays collections from pioneer days including many historic photographs.

Hatton (787) was named for the third assistant postmaster general at the time of its founding in 1882. Its locale is on the rich delta of ancient Elk River, a long-gone stream of Lake Agassiz days. Hatton's most famous native son was Carl Ben Eielson, the pioneer Alaskan aviator and Army Air Service pilot during World War I. Eielson learned his craft barnstorming across North Dakota in an airplane purchased by Hatton supporters. He was the first pilot to fly the mail into Alaska in 1922 and in 1928 made history by soaring across the top of the world in his Fokker high-wing monoplane with English explorer Sir Hubert Wilkins; the two teamed up again on several later Antarctic flights. Eielson died in 1929 while attempting to save the passengers and cargo of furs from the icebound ship Nanuk off North Cape, Siberia.

You can't miss Hatton's pride in his achievements. His 1926 Fokker airplane, the "Alaskan," is displayed in town. The archway

to St. John's Cemetery, which commemorates his flights, was purchased with North Dakota school children's pennies in 1931. Mementos of his life are displayed along with other pioneer artifacts and heirlooms in the Hatton-Eielson Museum. It occupies the old Andres Ness house, a historic Queen Anne-style residence built in 1910 and rescued in 1977 by the Hatton Historical Society; it is listed on the National Register of Historic Places. Hatton is also the home of two modern-day Norse institutions, Luther Bjerke, the homegrown humorist known as "the wild Norwegian of Beaver Creek," and Ole and Lena's Lefse. The latter's production of 10,000 lefses per day is concocted of area potatoes and marketed nationwide.

Larimore (1,524) borrowed its name from N.D. Larimore, a partner and business manager of Elk River Valley Farm, once said to be the world's largest under one

Pioneer aviator Carl Ben Eielson is honored in his hometown of Hatton where the house in which he grew up is now maintained as a museum and where he is buried not far from a memorial arch on Highway 18 north of the city. The museum hosts ice cream socials on selected summer weekends.

management with 15,000 acres. (Most bonanza farms were divided into more manageable units.) Owned by a land company in St. Louis, Mo., it was visited by St. Louis World's Fair Foreign Commission in 1904. The city has a pleasant park, and hiking trails wind through a shady arboretum along the reservoir of Larimore Dam just outside of town. The Larimore Community Museum displays collections of Sioux and Chippewa artifacts, bird eggs collected and catalogued by Thomas Eastgate, and military uniforms and weapons. It's open on summer Sundays.

Portland (627) stands on Campbell Beach, one of several laid down by glacial Lake Agassiz. It was once the home of Bruflat Academy, one of first private schools in state, established by local members of the Lutheran Church in 1889. Portland became a boom town with the railroad's arrival in 1881. The very Norwegian community was once noted for four its four progressive cooperatives — an oil company, grain elevator, creamery and store. This is the home of Gilman Rud, commander of the U.S. Navy's elite squadron of demonstration flyers, the Blue Angels.

Neighboring **Mayville** (2,255) was named for May Arnold, first white child born at the Hudson's Bay Trading Post established here in the 1870s. The town proper was begun in 1881 and moved to the railroad when it came through 1883. Mayville State College was established as teachers' college in 1889 and held its first classes 1893. Townspeople have come to the rescue of the small college time and again, from keeping its doors open with private donations in 1895 after the governor vetoed appropriations for all state colleges to 1970s and 1980s, when they again fought off attempts to close school or reconfigure it as a statewide science and mathematics high school.

Mayville was the home of etcher and photographer Levon West, better known as Ivan Dmitri. It was also the site of a 90-foot

(Top) The peaceful campus of Mayville State University. (Above) Keeping alive ethnic traditions, like these Norwegian singers from Mayville, is central to those who live in the predominantly Scandinavian Red River Valley. Visiting performers from the 'old country' are popular at community celebrations.

115

wooden ski jump built by the Goose River Ski Club and used for competitions by the largely Norwegian-American population. A smaller jump on a farm southeast of town was in use by the ski club until the early 1980s. Island Park is popular for picnics and summer recreation. The Goose River Heritage Center is located in the old Great Northern depot. Now on the National Register of Historic Places, the depot was preserved and renovated by the Mayville Pioneer Daughters. It's open, along with museum exhibits in the adjoining warehouse, on weekends throughout the summer.

Midway between Portland and Mayville is the ghost townsite of Traill Center, a legacy of the battle in 1883 to win the Traill County seat away from Hillsboro. If the supporters of the move had one, Mayville, Portland and Traill Center would have been merged into one. Interestingly, the number of ballots cast outnumbered legal voters by a substantial margin, and Traill Center won by a margin of five to one. To no one's surprise the election was contested. While it was in litigation, the territorial legislature abruptly transferred the two western tiers of townships from Traill to Steele County, sidelining Traill Center for all time.

Hillsboro (1,600) is one of many namesakes of James J. Hill, whose choice of this town rather than Caledonia for his Great Northern Railroad sealed its hopes and Caledonia's doom. It defended its county seat status not once but twice, beating back bids by both Traill Center and Caledonia. The Traill County Museum, located in the stately well-preserved 16-room brick Plummer home, exhibits articles related to the area's primarily Norwegian settlement along with Indian artifacts; it hosts an annual Old-Fashioned Fourth of July. Woodlawn Park, nestled in a horseshoe on the Goose River, offers a playground, swimming pool and extensive picnic facilities along with a venerable bandstand that once hosted weekly concerts by an

The quiet Goose River winds through lush farmland before spilling into the Red River at Caledonia. The valley is a haven for wildlife of all sorts.

outstanding community band. A flock of tame white geese now call the park and river home. Watch skies in this area for a glimpse of bright yellow Steerman Ag-Cat biplanes applying agricultural chemicals for Ron Deck's Sky Tractor Company.

Little remains of the prosperity that marked **Caledonia's** early years. Located at the confluence of the Goose and Red Rivers, it had big ideas until its fortunes abruptly turned. Tradition has it that James J. Hill came through by horse one blustery winter's night and was turned away by the local hotel. He went on to Hillsboro, vowing his revenge. The now-deserted site of **Belmont**, or Frog Point, is nearby on the banks of the Red River. When it became the head of steamboat navigation on the Red in 1872 it rapidly filled with trappers, boatmen, teamsters, drifters, saloonkeepers and dance-hall girls. Teamsters hauled freight overland from the south in heavy eight-horse high-wheeled "jumpers." Indians and trappers brought their furs to board the Hudson's Bay Co steamer *International* and James J. Hill's *Selkirk*. The wilderness metropolis gained fame even in Europe; foreign visitors from Fort Garry were reportedly disappointed not to spy a spired metropolis the equal of Liverpool. But the river level fell even further and the city dwindled and disappeared. An original log cabin from the Point now stands in Hillsboro's Woodlawn Park.

The townsite of **Buxton** (336) was owned by Bud Reeves, a politician who gained statewide fame by raising money for state colleges after their appropriation was vetoed in 1895. Reeves campaigned for Congress in '94 in what's believed to have been the very first house trailer — a log cabin built on wheels equipped with a large cowbell to announce his arrival. He spoke from its veranda, sharing it with an American flag and a live eagle. Other accomplished native sons include two governors, R.A. Nestos and A.G. Sorlie; U.S. Senator A.J. Gronna, the isolationist who opposed American entry into the First World War; and international banker and philanthropist Chester Fritz. The Buxton Historical Society has restored the Buxton State Bank, which is included in the National Register of Historic Places.

Reynolds (309) is distinguished by sitting half in Traill County and half in Grand Forks. It was named for Dr. Henry Reynolds, an impassioned advocate of temperance. Other Traill County towns include **Cummings**, **Blanchard** — near the KTHI-TV tower which, at 2,063 feet, is said to be tallest structure in North America, **Clifford**, **Galesburg** and **Kelso**.

Grand Forks lies just past **Thompson** (785) on Interstate 29. Now continue north of the city past **Kempton**, **McCanna** and

From an airplane, order can be made out of the patchwork of fields in the flat Red River Valley. Out on an inspection tour of his crops, this flying farmer passes over Golden Lake, a popular boating and fishing lake near Finley.

Honeyford. A gravel pit near town inters the mammoth but less-than-prehistoric remains of a circus elephant, the single casualty of a nearby train derailment. The beast's leg was broken in the accident; it was put out of its misery with a poisoned orange. Other nearby towns include **Orr, Gilby** (283) and **Inkster** (135).

Manvel (308) began as one of six stops on Fort Abercrombie-Fort Garry trail during the 1860s. The stage station was a crude log hut roofed with sod and later, a thriving thatch of weeds. Travelers got supper and spent the night on dirt floor for a modest 50 cents.

The **Warsaw** skyline is dominated by St. Stanislaus Catholic Church, in 1900 the largest in state and with the day's the largest congregation — 4,000 per Sunday. It was named after first Polish saint by the area's Polish settlers. This Cathedral of the Prairie was built in 1900, its entire $50,000 debt repaid within the next year. Today the much

smaller congregation's numbers still swell to hear the Polish choir on Easter and take part in midnight mass on Christmas Eve. The church was quickly rebuilt by its members after being gutted by fire in 1978.

Ardoch (78) is famed for Smokey's Steakhouse, the "home of the 54 oz. steak," chosen by *Midwest Living* Magazine as one of best steakhouses in Midwest. Boaters and anglers enjoy relaxing on nearby Lake Ardoch.

Minto (592) is named for an Ontario town, but was settled by Czechs and Poles who honor their roots with celebrations of the Feast of St. Wenceslaus on Sept. 28 and Czech Independence Day on Oct. 28. The Walsh County Historical Museum and Pioneer Village here are open on Sunday afternoons and summer holidays. Housed in a former schoolhouse, the museum includes a country store, blacksmith shop, ice cream parlor, pioneer home and wildlife displays. Outside

117

are an early jail, log cabin, country school and cook car.

Grafton (5,293) has several "firsts" to its credit — the first city in the Northwest with a municipal light plant, and the site of the first public library in North Dakota, established by a women's club in 1897. The city is the home of Grandma Campbell's Potato Chips, which manufactures 10,000 pounds of fresh crisp chips per month from white chipping potatoes grown on the Campbell brothers' 2,000 acres of spud fields. The Walsh Heritage Village here includes the Acton rural school, the Voss depot, the Landstad Church from Auburn, a log cabin more than 100 years old, a taxidermy shop and the local Little Theatre. The Grafton State School, an institution for the mentally retarded, was located here by the constitution but not opened until 1904. The institution was the target of a long, bitter lawsuit brought by the North Dakota Association for Retarded Citizens against the state in the mid-1970s over treatment and opportunities provided for its developmentally disabled residents. The population was greatly reduced as a result of deinstitutionalization, which has returned many former residents to communities around state.

North of Grafton along a country road is Jugville, the unique attraction created on their farm by Sig and Josie Jaglieski. A church, post office, country school and general store are comingled in the couple's private museum, along with farm machinery, a gazebo, flower gardens and enough artifacts to stock a respectable-sized historical society. Another Walsh County farmer, Henry French, sports a backyard landscaped with a 25-foot wooden saguaro cactus and an even taller concrete palm tree.

The unique Alexander Henry Rest Area on Interstate 29 south of Drayton may be the only highway rest stop to be outfitted with its own log palisade. It's near the spot where fur-trader Henry established a North West Company post in 1800. Henry's post became the site of the first non-Indian birth in North Dakota, a black child born to his servant Pierre Bonza. The first white child was also born here in 1807; he was the son of the "Orkney Lad," a woman masquerading as a male who worked at the post for several years. Her child's birth was the first sign that she was not all she seemed.

Drayton (1,082), named for a city in Ontario, is the only North Dakota town whose city park lies in another state. A drawbridge leads to the park across the river in Minnesota; it was built in 1911, when high water on Red River inspired hopes of reviving the steamboating industry. But the capricious river fell just as the bridge was completed. It has never risen as high again, and the bridge has never been lifted. Drayton has the oldest curling club in the state, established in 1904. The American Crystal Sugar Cooperative

Protected by shelterbelts, potatoes grown in the rich soil of the valley are world-renown for chipping and for baking. Much of the nation's supply of this valuable vitamin source is grown in the Red River Valley.

118

plant in Drayton processes sugarbeets grown in northeastern North Dakota and across the river. What some call the best fishing on the Red is reflected in the name of Catfish Haven Campground, which is outfitted with a bait shop and boat launch facilities.

Elsewhere in Walsh County, **Park River** (1,844) was named for so-called buffalo parks along river. Indian hunters herded the beasts into these brush corrals to await slaughter; they were often built beside a river or cliff so that animals could be driven over the edge and killed by the fall. One of several North Dakota Hutterite colonies is located in the surrounding countryside. Its members, of German origin, farm and live communally, observing strict codes of dress and behavior. Sinclair Lewis once owned a farm one mile from Park River, but he was never known to have visited it. William Avery Rockefeller, father of John D., lived on another Park River

farm for some time. The Standard Oil magnate purchased his land under the alias of Dr. William Levingston, who sold patent medicines and cancer treatments. Homme Dam near the city serves the dual purpose of providing recreation and flood control.

The Civic League of **Edinburg** (300) supports a local museum open on summer weekends. **Hoople** (350), the home of Governor Lynn J. Frazier, long reigned as one of the United States' primary potato shipment points. A pioneer log cabin dating from 1884 stands in the city park in **Adams** (303). Other area towns include **Nash**, **Fairdale** (97), **Lankin** (175), **Pisek** (156), **Voss**, **Forest River** (152), **Conway** (33) and **Fordville** (326).

If North Dakota were a giant platter, it would be tipped up at its southwest corner and down in Pembina County, the lowest point (at 790 feet above sea level) in the state.

The Red River courses by here toward its outlet in Hudson's Bay, occasionally wreaking havoc in area towns like **St. Thomas** (528) and **Bowesmont**. The latter was named for storekeeper William Bowes, who won the right to give the town his name in a heated card game. The former boasts two famous natives, Thomas E. Whalen, U.S. ambassador to Nicaragua under President Dwight Eisenhower, and Edward K. Thompson, editor of *Life* Magazine.

The name of **Joliette**, borrowed from a French-Canadian settlement in Quebec, reflects the French-Indian roots of many of area's original residents. Those roots began at **Pembina** (673), whose name is Chippewa for "highbush cranberry." The berry was a principle ingredient (along with dried meat and tallow) in pemmican, the high-energy trail food that fueled the voyageurs' and traders' forays into the land of the Red River. Charles Chaboillez built the first fur post on North Dakota soil in 1797-98 where the Pembina city park now stands. His competitors with the XY Company and Hudson's Bay Company built posts nearby in 1801. For the next 60 years Pembina was headquarters for the fur trade and, in the 1840s, the starting point of the last great Metis buffalo hunts.

The Pembina Historical Museum tells the story of the traders and of Lord Selkirk's starving Red River Colony, whose summer farming settlement here in 1812 kept the main colony at Winnipeg from starving through the bitter winters. The 1863 founding of the first Masonic lodge in what's now North Dakota is commemorated in Masonic Park, where Canadian and American flags fly side by side on Dominion Day and the Fourth of July. Since 1962 Pembina's largest employer, Motor Coach Industries, has assembled every passenger bus used by Greyhound and Trailways across the United States and Canada. The Pembina airport — occupying the site where the military Fort Pembina stood from 1870 to 1895 — was used by North

Located strategically near the Canadian border on I-29, the Alexander Henry Trading Post - really a rest area - is a popular stop for motorists. The rest area interprets the era of the fur trade which brought the first settlers to Pembina.

West Airlines in the 1930s as a major port of entry.

North Dakota's first homestead claim was filed on land in the vicinity in 1868 by Joseph Rolette, who'd arrived in 1842 with the American Fur Company and went on to become a leading member of the Minnesota Legislature. His claim was no small feat, since the nearest land office was in Vermilion, S.D.

A turn west onto N.D. Highway 5 leads to **Cavalier** (1,505), settled in 1875 by pioneers who arrived from Missouri in covered wagons. The party intended to relocate in Manitoba, but returned south of border after deciding they preferred the United States. Cavalier's Main Street follows the route of the old Fort Totten Trail. It has seen endless caravans of Red River oxcarts — as many as 1,500 in a single party — passing en route from Fort

Garry to St. Paul. The kink in the middle of Main Street originated when two adjoining landowners contributed the right of way — but failed to connect squarely. The Pembina County Museum here is open on summer Sundays. It shares the former bank and post office with the Cliff Jenson museum collection and the Pioneer Daughters' museum.

Hamilton is the site of the oldest bank in the state, established by Dakota Territory charter in 1886. (Mayville's Goose River State Bank was created that same year.) In honor of the Bank of Hamilton, residents have given it the official address of Number One Wall Street.

Icelandic State Park is not far from **Backoo**, a town named by settler John Mountain for the Barcoo River in his native Australia, and now the home of the No Place Saloon. The state park is a popular center for outdoor enthusiasts from throughout northeastern North Dakota, with its swimming beach on Lake Renwick along with boating and fishing for northern pike; and oak-shaded picnic facilities and campgrounds. The Wildwood Nature Trail (designated a National Recreational Trail) meanders through Gunlogson Arboretum Nature Preserve, a 200-acre naturally wooded area along the Tongue River. More than a dozen rare species of plants and animals are found here, from the southern watermeal (one of the world's smallest flowering plants) to the bizarre-looking pileated woodpecker.

Sharing the Gunlogson homestead site is the Pioneer Heritage Center under development for the centennial. The early homestead buildings are to be joined by other historic buildings — Akra Hall, Cranley School, Hallson Church and the John Eastman Farm and Cabin — as well as a new interpretive center and amphitheatre for the popular naturalist programs. Rich in cultural and natural history, benefactor G.B. Gunlogson said the area embraced "a living story about how the land was formed by glaciers, water,

Northeastern North Dakota is blessed with wooded hills that on good years almost rivals New England for the beauty of the turning leaves. (Top) The Gunlogson Arboretum near Cavalier has miles of hiking trails through the trees along the Tongue River.

wind, plant growth and time." Hiking and cross-country skiing trails lead through elm and basswood forest into shallow woodland ponds and damp thickets, under the watchful eye of birds both rare and common.

Akra — Icelandic for "fields" — stands on the edge of old Lake Agassiz. Other Icelandic towns include **Hallson** (the oldest), **Mountain** (156), **Svold** and **Gardar**. These Icelanders arrived in America in 1874, settling in Gimli, Man.; over the next four years they gradually returned a thousand miles south, choosing the rugged terrain of Little Tongue River headwaters. A log church built in 1886 near **Mountain** (156) is said to be the oldest Icelandic church in North America. The area is the home of Arctic explorer Vinhjalmur Stefansson.

The little town of **Hensel** (68) possesses not one but two official names. The settlement was incorporated as Canton Village, but the post office a mile away adopted the name Hensel. The two eventually consolidated, each retaining its old legal identity.

Concrete (south on N.D. 89) is the site of a cement mine operated from 1907 to 1909 near the source of Tongue River. Mining came to a close when the price of imported cement dipped below the domestic product. The region also has deposits of Fuller's earth.

The Pembina Gorge six miles west of Walhalla on the Pembina River dips low rather than swoops high above the surrounding prairie. Carved by melting glacial waters, it represents one of the longest and deepest river valleys of North Dakota. Elk and moose live among its trees, which blaze with color in autumn. Its slopes offer downhill and cross country skiing in winter. Tetrault Woods State Forest just south of Walhalla typifies the area, with its 480 species of plants, its elk herd and 75 species of breeding birds. The forest has trails for hiking, horsebackriding, all-terrain vehicles and cross-country skiing.

Father G.A. Belcourt established St. Joseph's Mission near the future site of **Walhalla** (1,429) in 1848, serving the area's Chippewa people. Its intricately molded Angelus Bell was brought downriver by boat, then overland by ox cart. The area evolved into an important fur trading post; after furs became scarce and buffalo disappeared, so did the first town. The Walhalla area was the home of Metis fur trader and prominent Minnesota territorial legislator Antoine Gingras. His log cabin (built in 1847) and the nearby trading post have been restored as a state historic site. The first wheat exported from North Dakota — by ox cart — was grown on a farm near Walhalla by Charles Bottineau.

The settlement of Walhalla was revived and replatted by mostly Scandinavian settlers in 1877 and renamed Walhalla, the home of the gods in Norse mythology. Dawn Enterprises established an ethanol plant here in the mid-1980s to manufacture ethanol from the local barley harvest. The project was guaranteed a troubled future due to hot debate over whether gasoline with ethanol as an additive is safe for use in automobiles. Frost Fire Mountain ski area six miles west of Walhalla draws downhill skiers with seven runs. It is the only ski area in North Dakota equipped with chair lifts; it also boasts a chalet with a snack bar and equipment rental. Cross-country ski trails and

Downhill skiing is a prime winter activity at Frost Fire Mountain near Walhalla. Snowmobiling and cross-country skiing are also popular. In the fall, the Pembina Hills become North Dakota's premier hunting area.

snowmobile trails are also available throughout the area. The Walhalla Historic Site/Old Settlers Park nearby maintains the site of Alexander Henry's 1801 trading post and Kittson House, built in 1841 as a trading post and warehouse under the direction of Norman Kittson, the first postmaster in North Dakota history and a power in Minnesota Territory politics. Other Pembina County towns include **Leroy**, an old settlement that was the center of the local Meti community, and **Neche** (471), whose name is Chippewa for "friend."

Bathgate (67), a quiet little town nestled along the Tongue River, was the original site of the State School for Blind, which from 1908 until the 1960s educated blind youngsters from throughout the state. It was moved to Grand Forks for easier access to medical care, higher education and transportation; its building is now Memorial Pioneer Rest Home.

Langdon (2,335) was at first known as McHugh for Patrick McHugh, one of first county commissioners, a territorial legislator and a member of state constitutional convention. He obtained free right-of-way for the Great Northern to extend its line from Park River to Langdon in 1887; the company thanked him with the townsites of **Edinburg**, Milton, Osnabrock and McHugh. But his namesake city was renamed a short while later after the surveyor and contractor of the Great Northern branch line, Mr. Langdon, who said "thank you" to the village with the gift of a bell for its new school.

Langdon and nearby **Nekoma** (102) boomed during the late 1960s and early 1970s when the nation's $5.7 billion Minutemen II system was built in the area. The ABM (anti-ballistic missile) program brought unprecedented growth to the region until 1975, when it was decommissioned immediately after its completion as a part of President Richard Nixon's detente negotiations with the Soviet Union. Today underground missile sites dot wheatfields of northern North Dakota.

Pyramids atop deeply planted radar and control facilities peer at the world in Nekoma, whose name is Chippewa for "I promise." The state's search for other occupants of the costly defense installation has turned up candidates ranging from a rehabilitation program for wayward teens to a mushroom farm.

Dresden is the site of the Cavalier County Historical Society's museum complex, which includes a log cabin from the Olga-Vang area, a fieldstone Catholic church on its original site, a one-room country schoolhouse from rural Langdon and a new building with seven period rooms depicting pioneer enterprises. It's open on summer Sundays. A wildlife sanctuary is operated near **Rock Lake** (287), which marks a turn in the route onto U.S. 281. The Towner County Historical Museum at **Egeland** (112) houses settlers' memorabilia along with farm equipment and

vehicles. Larsen's Blacksmith Shop and the original fieldstone jail stand on its grounds.

The name of **Cando** (1,496) emerged from a heated county commission debate in 1884. Chairman P.P. Parker: "There has been much talk about our not having power to locate this county seat where we see fit. But we'll show you that we can do it. And furthermore, just to show you what we can do, we'll name this county seat 'Can-Do.'" The Cando Pioneer Foundation has renovated the old First State Bank, in which it maintains exhibits on the area's history. Cando is the unofficial capital of North Dakota's Durum Triangle, which produces some 85 percent of the crop grown in the entire United States. It's also the site of Noodles by Leonardo, established in 1981 by Minneapolis developer Leonard Gasparre, and now employing 250 full-time workers. His pasta's key ingredient

It is now a quiet, peaceful, yet eerie place - the decommissioned anti-ballistic missile site near Nekoma. Rising up from nearby wheat fields, the radar site intended to warn of nuclear war was a super-power bargaining chip which closed immediately after achieving readiness. A small maintenance crew still works on the site.

is semolina from durum grown here and milled at the State Mill in Grand Forks. The firm markets its products under private labels and its own premium brand nationwide. Cando author Judy Baer has written many romance novels for Zondervan and other national publishers.

Maza (21) is located near Lac aux Mortes/Lake Alice, wildlife refuge. The lake's French name comes from the sight of Indian victims of smallpox epidemic in early 1860s. As was the custom, survivors placed their corpses high in trees along the lake, visible for miles against the sky. The woods were later destroyed by prairie fire.

Other Cavalier County towns include **Hannah** (90), **Sarles** (111), whose name honors North Dakota's first governor E.Y. Sarles, **Wales** (74) where Welsh settler took up claims, **Calio** (60), **Alseth** and **Mount Carmel** — named by a Catholic missionary to the Indians for Palestine's Mount Carmel, where the Order of Our Lady of Mount Carmel was founded in the 12th century. A nearby German Catholic settlement of Mount Moriah was absorbed by Carmel.

Like Dresden, **Munich** (300) reflects the homeland of early German settlers. **Maida** may have been named after the hunting dog of two visiting Canadian bankers, whom they felt resembled the canine lead in a book by Sir Walter Scott. Historians agree that **Olga** was a Norwegian princess, and **Osnabrock** (222) the Ontario city from which its first postmaster came. **Milton** (195) was named for English poet John Milton, who once visited and hunted in the Red River Valley. There's little mystery about why **Union** was so designated by its first settler, a blue-garbed veteran of the Civil War; it's one of 50 American cities to share the name. But the reason why **Loma** (39) is named (in Spanish) for "broad-topped hill" remains a mystery. The land is flat here. III

Farmers add to the beauty of northeastern North Dakota by planting colorful sunflowers. In many cases, trees are the best crop that can be grown on the heavily wooded hillsides.

Index

Russ Hanson, Nancy Edmonds Hanson, Sheldon Green

Nancy Edmonds Hanson is a frequent contributor to *North Dakota Horizons* and other regional and national magazines, and is director of public relations with Hetland Ltd. of Fargo. Raised in Hillsboro and Streeter, she has written two national best-selling guides for freelance writers; produced a weekly news program for statewide public television; edited a variety of periodicals, and founded Prairie House, a publisher of regional books. The former Fargo *Forum* reporter and assistant state travel director attended Concordia College and graduated from Moorhead State University in 1971.

Sheldon Green is the editor of *North Dakota Horizons* Magazine. A native of Hatton, he graduated from the University of North Dakota in 1971. He was editor of the Hazen Star for ten years during the time of coal conversion development in western North Dakota. Green has also worked for daily newspapers in Idaho and Green Bay, Wisconsin, where he developed and edited a weekend magazine supplement. His writing, photography and design have won several awards and his work has appeared in national publications. He lives with his wife and family in Bismarck.

Russ Hanson is director of photography with Hetland Ltd. of Fargo. Formerly chairman of Bismarck Junior College's graphic arts department, the Mandan native has contributed photographs to a long list of state, regional and national books and periodicals, from *North Dakota Horizons* to *Midwest Living* to National Geographic Books. He is a 1968 graduate of BJC and earned his degree in photography and cinematography from Southern Illinois University in 1970. He, his wife Nancy and their daughter Patti live in Fargo-Moorhead.

127

North Dakota Centennial Book Series

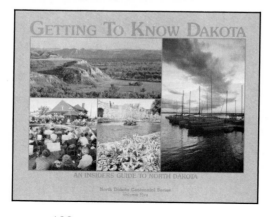

North Dakota Centennial Book Series

A beautiful, informative and visually graphic series of softbound books that honors North Dakota's first 100-years.

Each volune contains 128-pages, with over 200 color photographs with an easy-reading text that provides an entertaining mix of history, anecdotes, tall tales and frontier stories.

Volume One: *'Cross the Wide Missouri.* The counties that border the Missouri River and Lake Sakakawea.

Volume Two: *Bread Basket of the World.* The agricultural wealth of the Red River Valley.

Volume Three: *Heart of the Prairie.* The prairie pothole country and the most varied scenery in the state.

Volume Four: *Sagebrush, Buttes and Buffalo.* The rugged beauty of the Badlands and the colorful characters of the past.

Volume Five: *Getting to Know Dakota.* Just in time for your trip back home for the Centennial. An insider's guide to our scenic, historic and recreational places. Easy to follow tours are suggested, accompanied by informative maps and beautiful photography. A book to be treasured for years . . . and an ideal gift!

All volumes are $17.45 each (includes shipping & handling).